Reactive Programming with Angular and ngrx

Learn to Harness the Power of
Reactive Programming with RxJS
and ngrx Extensions

Oren Farhi

apress®

Reactive Programming with Angular and ngrx: Learn to Harness the Power of Reactive Programming with RxJS and ngrx Extensions

Oren Farhi
Lod, Israel

ISBN-13 (pbk): 978-1-4842-2619-3   ISBN-13 (electronic): 978-1-4842-2620-9
DOI 10.1007/978-1-4842-2620-9

Library of Congress Control Number: 2017941328

Managing Director: Welmoed Spahr
Editorial Director: Todd Green
Acquisitions Editor: Louise Corrigan
Development Editor: James Markham
Technical Reviewer: Luca Mezzalira
Coordinating Editor: Nancy Chen
Copy Editor: April Rondeau
Artist: SPi Global

Distributed to the book trade worldwide by Springer Science+Business Media New York, 233 Spring Street, 6th Floor, New York, NY 10013. Phone 1-800-SPRINGER, fax (201) 348-4505, e-mail orders-ny@springer-sbm.com, or visit www.springeronline.com. Apress Media, LLC is a California LLC and the sole member (owner) is Springer Science + Business Media Finance Inc. (SSBM Finance Inc.). SSBM Finance Inc is a **Delaware** corporation.

For information on translations, please e-mail rights@apress.com, or visit http://www.apress.com/rights-permissions.

Apress titles may be purchased in bulk for academic, corporate, or promotional use. eBook versions and licenses are also available for most titles. For more information, reference our Print and eBook Bulk Sales web page at http://www.apress.com/bulk-sales.

Any source code or other supplementary material referenced by the author in this book is available to readers on GitHub via the book's product page, located at www.apress.com/9781484226193. For more detailed information, please visit http://www.apress.com/source-code.

Printed on acid-free paper

This book is dedicated to the love of my life, Adi, for always supporting me and allowing me to move forward; to my lovely kids, I hope this will inspire you in your ways; to my mother and father for loving me unconditionally; and to my entire supportive family.

Contents at a Glance

Contents

About the Author

Oren Farhi is a Senior Front End Engineer and JavaScript Consultant at Orizens (http://orizens.com). He consults to companies on how to approach front-end development and create maintainable code as well as on front-end project development by demand.

He studied Computer Science and Management at The Open University, Israel.

Oren believes in producing easily maintainable code for applications by following the principles of reactive programming, best practices of software architecture and by creating modular testable code. He likes to keep the code and app structure organized so as to let other developers easily understand and extend it.

Oren is proficient with JavaScript and front-end development. He works with various solutions, such as Angular, ngrx, react, redux, sass, webpack, jasmine, nodejs, and JavaScript–based Build Tools, which solve challenges well.

Aside from exploring web development and blogging, Oren enjoys spending time with his family, playing guitar, meditating, traveling, and watching TV series and movies.

About the Technical Reviewer

Luca Mezzalira is an Italian solutions architect with thirteen years of experience, a Google Developer Expert on web technologies, and the manager of the London JavaScript community (www.londonjs.uk). He has worked on cutting-edge projects for mobile (iOS, Android, Blackberry), desktop, web, TVs, set-top boxes, and embedded devices.

He believes the best way to use any programming language is by mastering its models, and thus spends much of his time studying and researching topics like OOP, functional programming, and reactive programming. With these skills, he's able to switch easily between different programming languages, applying the best practices he learned and driving any team to success.

In his spare time, he's written for national and international technical magazines. He has also tech reviewed for Packt Publishing, Pragmatic Bookshelf, and O'Reilly.

He was a speaker at the following: O'Reilly media webinars, O'Reilly Solutions Architect (San Francisco), O'Reilly Oscon (London), Voxxed Days (Belgrad), JSDay (Verona), CybercomDev (Łódź), Jazoon Conference (Bern), JDays (Göteborg), Codemotion (Milan), FullStack Conference (London), React London UG (London), Node London UG (London), Scrum Gathering (Prague), Agile Cymru (Cardiff), Scotch on the Rocks (Edinburgh & London), 360Max (San Francisco), PyCon (Florence), Lean Kanban Conference (London), Flash Camp (Milan), Adobe Creative Suite CS 5.5 Launch event (Milan), HFWAA (Milan, Turin, Padua, Bari, Florence), and Mobile World Congress (Barcelona).

Introduction

This book is designed to be followed by a working code example application. The application is a lite version of an open source media player—Echoes Player. The full version of the Echoes Player source code is available on its github repository at http://github.com/orizens/echoes-player.

The Angular version used in this book is aimed at the second generation of the framework—starting from version 2.0.0 and up and simply noted as "Angular" (as opposed to the first version, "AngularJS"). Angular uses now semantic versioning (semver), which means that each version has a meaning, as noted in Table 1.

Table 1. Semantic Versioning (semver) Meaning

4	0	1
Major (breaking changes)	**Minor** (new features, no breaking changes)	**Patch** (bug fixes, no breaking changes)

The `ngrx/store` used in this book refers to version 2.2.1. At the time of writing this book, there were some discussions about the next major version—3.0.0. As it appears from the github issues of `ngrx/store`, version 3 should add enhancements and some fixes. There might be a change in bootstrapping the store's module; however, the main interface for dispatching and selecting the store's state should stay the same.

The `ngrx/effects` used in this book refers to version 2. At the time of writing this book, there were no discussions of the next major version.

Starting with Chapter 2, each chapter's sample code is available in a dedicated branch. For example, in order to switch to Chapter 2's source code, you need to check out the `chapter-02` branch.

These are the available branches for each chapter:

1. Chapter 2 - git checkout **chapter-02**

2. Chapter 3 - git checkout **chapter-03**

3. Chapter 4 - git checkout **chapter-04**

4. Chapter 5 - git checkout **chapter-05**

5. Chapter 6 - git checkout **chapter-06**

6. Chapter 7 - git checkout **chapter-07**

Each chapter's branch includes the final code updates that were reviewed and shown during the chapter.

■ **Note**   Please remember to run `npm install` when switching branches, as some branches introduce new `npm` packages.

You can find the companion website for this book at `http://orizens.com/wp/angular-ngrx-book/`.

CHAPTER 1

■ ■ ■

Getting Started with the Echoes Player Lite App

Welcome to our journey into the reactive programming world with Angular. You are going to build a web application using Angular, ngrx modules, and reactive programming concepts.

You may have experience with AngularJS, and you may have heard that Angular is completely different. You may have experience in other MV* frameworks and want to get into the world of reactive programming using Angular. In either case, I'm sure your experience will be handy.

In this chapter, we lay the groundwork for building a web application that is capable of running on any browser that Angular supports. This is usually the latest A-grade browser, but might include backward compatibility in older versions. Here, I cover subjects such as getting familiar with the final product, understanding the structure of the application and its architecture, and getting familiar with the reactive extension that will be used in the final app.

Browser and Development Environment

We'll work with Chrome and its Developer Tools panel. Chrome is defined as an A-grade browser and follows the latest standards of the web.

■ **Note**   All examples in this book are displayed using Chrome. However, it is possible to run the application on other modern A-grade browsers.

Augury Dev Tools Extension

Augury is an extension available for the Developer Tools panel (currently available for Chrome only). Its main purpose is to assist in debugging and inspecting Angular applications.

© Oren Farhi 2017
O. Farhi, *Reactive Programming with Angular and ngrx*,
DOI 10.1007/978-1-4842-2620-9_1

A full description and an installation link can be found on its home page: `https://augury.angular.io/`.

After installing the extension via the Chrome web store, when you open an Angular application in development mode in the browser, you can open the Developer Tools panel and switch to the new panel, Augury, at which point you will see the panel shown in Figure 1-1.

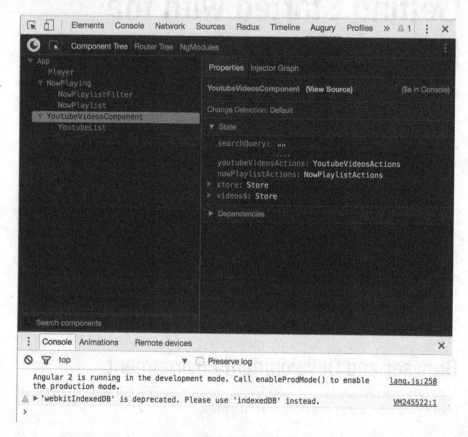

Figure 1-1. Augury panel in Chrome's Developer Tools panel

Augury provides the following benefits when developing with Angular:

- It outlines the application as a tree of Angular components.

- When a component is selected, its properties can be viewed and edited in the right-hand panel.

- An injector graph visualizes the inject tree.

- You can search for a specific component and show HTML elements.

Version Control and Deployment

When we create applications, we'll work off a boilerplate. We'll make changes and updates to the files and folders. It is a good idea to use some sort of a version-control system.

I usually work with git. It saves everything locally and is widely supported by Cloud services, such as Github, Bitbucket, and GitLab, so you could easily use it for online backup as well. However, any other version-control system will do, like mercurial, svn, or another option.

As for deployment, in both Github and Bitbucket you can host a static web server and run the application on the Cloud. From there, there are many options with which to automate the deployment process as well as run unit tests and connect to other services.

If you don't know either service, I suggest you pick Github. It's easy to install and configure for one of the Cloud providers.

Setting the Development Environment

The development environment in Angular is based on node.js, which is an open source, cross-platform JavaScript runtime environment. Its interpreter engine uses Google's V8 JavaScript engine.

Node.js has many built-in modules, sometimes referred to as packages. Aside from the built-in modules, there are thousands of modules that can be installed using node's package manager, npm (https://npmjs.com). npm has other uses, including running scripts for deployment and running unit tests.

Angular is a framework that is composed of npm modules that can be installed via npm.

In the next chapters, we'll use npm several times in order to run some build tasks through the terminal (or command line, in Windows). In fact, using npm should be second nature when developing web applications today, as it simplifies both the development process and preparing for production. I'm sure that by the time you hit the end of this book, you'll be familiar with some of the capabilities of npm.

Instructions on how to install node.js can found at https://nodejs.org.

Terminal/Command Line

As explained before, in order to run npm scripts, you'll need a terminal or a command line. Any operating system is packaged with one.

There are few differences between a terminal and a command line, which are used in Linux and Windows, respectively. However, usually we'll interact with npm scripts, which act as an adapter between those platforms, and usually, if used with the right tools, npm abstracts the usage in each operating system.

If you'd like to work with a Linux-like terminal in Windows, ConEmu emulates the Linux terminal, and other terminals as well, and can found at https://conemu.github.io/.

Editor (IDE or Code Editor)

The editor is where you'll do all your work developing the application. Angular is written with Typescript, though you can use plain JavaScript as well. If you choose to go with Typescript, it's beneficial if you choose a Typescript-aware editor.

Some of the benefits of using such an editor are the following:

1. Code auto-completion

2. Display errors (if there are any) as you type

3. Easy navigation within the code

4. Assistance in importing modules

Code editors that I've worked with while developing with Angular and that I can recommend are as follows:

1. Sublime Text – http://www.sublimetext.com/

2. Atom.io (by Github) – https://atom.io/

3. Visual Studio Code (By Microsoft) – https://code.
    visualstudio.com/

These editors are cross-platform. They support Mac, Windows, and Linux. There are more editors and IDEs that can be used for Angular development as well, including WebStorm.

Application Structure

After your computer is set up with the recommended tools, you're ready to go ahead and start building the application. But before we write any code, as with any other process, it is wise to stop for a few moments and think.

Once we understand the base structure and fundamentals, it will be easier for us to understand where to add new code and how to approach a new feature.

The Angular application structure follows some best practices, which are described in the formal Angular style guide, found at the documentation website at https://angular.io/docs/ts/latest/guide/style-guide.html. It is also derived from the application boilerplate that this project is based on—AngularClass's angular2-webpack-starter at https://github.com/AngularClass/angular-starter. I'll dive into this boilerplate later in a dedicated chapter.

I chose to adjust the structure a little bit so that learning to locate domain-specific files (logics, actions, services, core app files, etc.) will be easy.

Since we're going to use ngrx/store as a state-management solution with Angular, it is important to get familiar with the structure of the app.

The application is illustrated in Figure 1-2 and consists of the following main parts:

- **App** – the main app directory; includes all the app files

- **Assets & Styles** – files and directories that are located relatively to the app's root directory that will run in development mode.

- **App Files** – files that define the main app and are the only files without a directory under the app directory (i.e., app.routes.ts, app.html index.ts, etc.)

- **Components (container)** – A directory that includes components that wraps presentational components and is often responsible for fetching data with services; orchestrates between several other components; interacts with the core app. Often referred as Smart Components.

- **Core** – A directory that includes any fundamental modules (functions, components, or other) that should be consumed by Container Components. The core services, state, side effects, and others have their own directories inside the core directory.

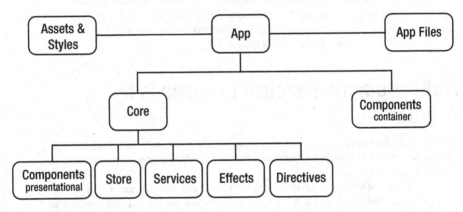

Figure 1-2. *The parts of the application*

The following are Core directories:

- **Components (presentational)** – Often referred as "dumb" components or "stateless" components, these are logic-less components that concern how to render data that are given to them. Sometimes, these components may notify of certain interesting events (by emitting events) that might influence new or updated data, cause a chain reaction to other events, as so on. Any component that should be available to other developers that want to develop a container component should reside here. Such components may be Grid, Dropdown, Tabs, User Profile Card, and so forth.

- **Store** – This directory defines the one and only store, which holds the state of the application. With this special module, we're able to build the foundation for neat and clean reactive programming (Redux). Alongside this definition, there are going to be function reducers that alter this state or part of it, actions, and action creators (we'll look at this in more depth later in a dedicated chapter and explain what Redux is).

5

- **Effects** – This is another important foundation of reactive programming. Simply put, sometimes an action involves side effects that need handling in some manner (a chain reaction). A good example is a situation where the user clicks on a button to save, a "saving..." animation is then shown in response to the request that has been initialized, and after save is completed and the response has been returned to the client, the "saved!" notification is shown.

- **Services** – this directory includes application-wide services and is responsible for creating requests to external services (usually backend microservices). These can be Authorization, Searching, REST APIs, Websockets, and much more.

- **Directives** – these are application-wide directives that should be available to Container Components, much like Tabs and Grid. A good example is the Draggable directive, which enhances any element/component with a drag ability.

RxJS and ngrx: Reactive Extensions for Angular

Angular includes the RxJS library as a development dependency. RxJS is essentially a "toolbox" library that includes functions that eventually allow us to program code using a functional approach.

ngrx is a set of libraries that uses the concepts of reactive programming and uses the RxJS library to implement it. It includes libraries that provide state management (ngrx/store), side-effects management (ngrx/effects), integration of routing to state management (ngrx/router-store), and more.

RxJS

RxJS is based on the concept of streams—objects that hold data, while over time this data may be updated or changed. Usually, we would like to perform some action when this data changes, or *react* to these changes by performing one action or more.

■ **Note** A stream of data might be updated synchronously or asynchronously, while the notification of the data update will occur right after the operation.

RxJS includes the concept of *operators*, or functions, which are the main tools for dealing with streams of data, transforming it, processing it, and achieving complex tasks with just a few lines of code.

One of the main concepts in RxJS is that of an *observable*. Usually, an observable is a collection of values that may be updated over time. This means that this collection can be observed by an *observer*—a collection of callbacks—which will be invoked whenever the data is changed. To simplify this idea, you can think of it as a very powerful "Event Bus." You can register to events, deregister from events, and trigger events, quite the same as you would on a regular Event Bus. However, at any step in these operations, you can define an operator function in order to combine, filter, and create new events at any time. This is actually the operation of looking at a stream of data (or better: observing) and performing actions to alter that stream to the application's needs.

There's much more to RxJS than I have described thus far. It is greater than the scope of this book and deserves its own fully dedicated book. However, as we progress in developing and understanding reactive programming with Angular and ngrx libraries, we will get more familiar with a few of the main concepts and building blocks of RxJS.

ngrx: Reactive Extensions for Angular

ngrx is a set of reactive-oriented modules for Angular. It aims to provide common features for the Angular platform by leveraging reactive programming concepts, with RxJS at its core.

In this book, we'll get to know a few of these features while integrating ngrx into our application.

ngrx/core

The core is a library that all ngrx modules are based on. As its name suggests, it includes core reactive-style operators and utilities. These are based on RxJS operators and expose a high-level API to assist with creating reactive objects for use with the Angular platform.

ngrx/store

The store is a state-management solution inspired by the famous library *Redux*. Redux popularized the idea of organizing the application state into simple objects (use primitive and non-primitive types in JavaScript) and updating this state by replacing it with a new state. This means that the object shouldn't be mutated directly, but rather should be replaced with a new state object.

The store instance is a singleton data object. You can think of it as a database that you can get access to in order to retrieve or update the data that the application operates on.

In order to update data in the store (a state), we can use the *dispatch* method. This method takes an action argument (a string) and a second optional data argument of any type. This method actually triggers an event (remember Event Bus?) that will handle those functions that are registered (we'll get into it in depth in a later chapter).

The event that has been triggered by the dispatch method should be handled by a *reducer*—a pure function. A reducer function should receive two arguments, as follows:

1. State

2. Action

The State argument is the actual current data state.

The Action argument is an object that includes only two properties—type and payload. Type is required and is usually a string that represents the event type that this reducer should handle. Payload is a property that can hold any type of data relevant to the action that should be handled.

A reducer function should not mutate the State argument directly, but rather "derive" the data from it and create a new state, which will be returned as the new state value and as the return value of this function. This kind of function is very easy to test since the output becomes predictable once the input arguments are known.

Since by nature JavaScript objects are mutable, you should stick to the convention of not mutating the state object, or use a third-party library to enforce the state's being immutable.

■ **Note** A *pure function* is defined as pure as long as it outputs the same value given the same input arguments, and as long as it doesn't mutate any value outside its scope or cause any side effects. It aids in predictability and ease in writing simple unit tests.

---

ngrx/effects

The ngrx/effects module is essentially a factory with which to create a side effect model for ngrx/store. Sometimes, a certain action should be followed by another action.

Usually, a side effect happens when an asynchronous operation starts. For example, take a simple HTTP request to retrieve data. In this case, the UI should indicate that this operation is in process, and when it's completed the UI should display the new data, and perhaps this new data will cause a few UI changes.

There are at least two actions that happen here:

1. A Start Data retrieve action

2. A Success (completed) Data action

Both actions can be defined in this case as a change in state. We know this is true because the state alters what is displayed in the UI.

I like to think of ngrx/effects as a layer that groups several actions as a specific chain of reactions. This leads to organize the code in such a way that the logics for side effects are placed in a dedicated directory- "effects" - while services are managed separatley in the "services" directory.

ngrx/store-log-monitor

This module is actually a developer tool extension. It's a little bit different from the previous modules. Its aim is to assist in development with the previous "ngrx" extensions. The "ngrx/store-log-monitor" a port of redux devtools log monitor.

It adds a panel to Chrome's Developer Tools. This new panel displays the current state and logs any action that has been triggered, along with its data. You can also interact with this panel to actually "go back in time" to any previous state that has been logged. This is a very powerful extension that can assist in debugging and trace an action flow once it has been triggered.

In the last chapter, I show the steps required to connect this module to the application that we build so we can see how it can leverage the debug process.

The Sample Application

Throughout this book's chapters we will create a real application while getting to know reactive programming with Angular and ngrx modules.

The application is Echoes Player (Lite). It's a lite version of an open source application that I developed with AngularJS and Angular. The app consumes YouTube's data API to allow searching for videos and playlists. YouTube Player (an iframe) is also used to allow the playback of videos. Finally, we'll authenticate users with the Google Sign-in API and retrieve the user's YouTube playlists.

I started developing this application as a way to explore Angular's libraries and in order to have a playground for experimenting with several features and ideas. It also gives me the opportunity to develop with my favorite tools while listening to music—the best of both worlds.

You can navigate to the real application at http://orizens.github.io/echoes/. Figure 1-3 is a screenshot of the live production application, developed with AngularJS.

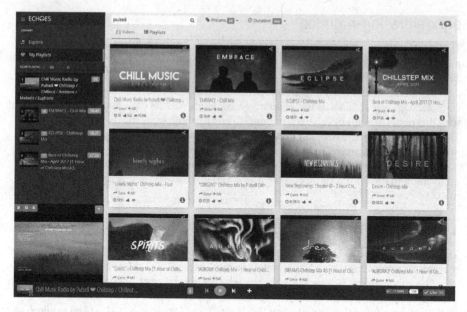

Figure 1-3. *Echoes Player with Angular 1 (`http://orizens.github.io/echoes/`)*

Figure 1-4 is a screenshot of the application created with Angular. It's a little bit different than AngularJS version.

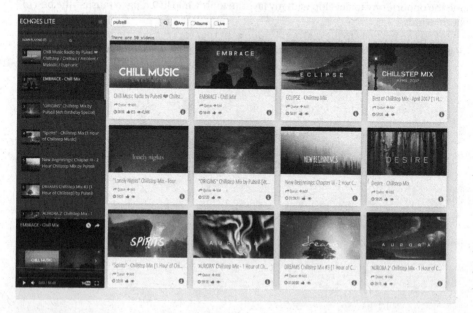

Figure 1-4. *Echoes Player with Angular (`http://orizens.github.io/echoes-player`)*

Summary

In this chapter, I introduced the development environment, the tools that we can work with when developing with Angular, the libraries that we will work with, and the Echoes Player application that we will build with these tools. You should now have a full working development environment and an understanding of the basic concepts.

In the next chapter, we are going to get familiar with the code boilerplate that the Echoes Player application will be based on. This will give us a bird's eye view of the project structure as well as of the build tools that are used to run the development environment, the testing environment, and the production build process.

CHAPTER 2

■ ■ ■

Getting Familiar with Boilerplate for Development

Nowadays, it's quite common to jumpstart a development project by modifying an existing one. Starting out in this way gives you a head start and can speed up the development process.

In this chapter, we'll create a sample application, Echoes Player (Lite), to be used throughout the book to demonstrate the various assets of Angular and ngrx tools. Echoes Player starts from a boilerplate made by the AngularClass team (https://angularclass.com/) and is based on the official boilerplate of the Angular 2 Webpack starter (https://github.com/AngularClass/angular2-webpack-starter).

We'll go into detail on the following subjects:

- Structure overview

- The world of Webpack tooling

- The development and deployment workflow

■ **Note** Webpack is a module bundler mainly used for web development. It creates a dependency graph from any files that have been loaded by a proper loader plugin so that those files can be imported into other files using any form of module loading. It is also used for bundling a production-ready version for deployment.

Before we begin, though, it's important to understand the boilerplate's underlying principles, along with the libraries and tools that are included with it and how they can assist us during development.

Boilerplate Overview

The structure of a project is organized into a well-defined set of directories and files. The dependencies of this boilerplate are indicated in the package.json file. However, aside from tracking the dependencies, package.json includes the *scripts* section—tasks that can be run with npm in the terminal.

© Oren Farhi 2017
O. Farhi, *Reactive Programming with Angular and ngrx*,
DOI 10.1007/978-1-4842-2620-9_2

This boilerplate's package.json file includes quite a few ordered scripts that we can interact with; however, we will only use a few of these. Some scripts use other scripts with a switch, some are relevant for production or testing mode, while others are relevant for several development modes. We'll interact with some of these scripts later in this book.

Looking at the directories structure (Figure 2-1), we can see that on the first level of the project there are only two directories: config and src. Let's take a high-level look at them and their contents now.

Figure 2-1. *Directories structure for this book's boilerplate*

The "config" directory

The config directory includes the main build and deploy code as part of its tools. The config files for Webpack (the build tool that is being used) can be found here.

There are three main config files for Webpack. Each is destined for an environment that will be run and compiled by Webpack:

1. development config – webpack.dev.js

2. production config – webpack.prod.js

3. test config – webpack.test.js

There is also a webpack.common.js file, since there are common configuration settings that all of these environments consume.

■ **Note** The gh-pages branch in Github serves as a static web server. For example, the Echoes Player ng2 project can be accessed through `http://orizens.github.io/echoes-player`. The source files are served from `http://github.com/orizens/echoes-player/tree/gh-pages`.

There are also other configuration files, including tests configuration files for unit tests run using Karma and an end-to-end configuration file for protractor. Since we will experiment with writing unit tests, let's review Karma's configuration file.

Karma

Karma is a node.js package that can be installed using npm:

```
npm install karma --save-dev
```

Customizing Karma with Configuration

Karma's plugins, adapters, and preprocessors are also node modules that can be installed via the npm registry.

Karma is configurable via the karma.conf.js file. There are a few settings that we can configure in this file in order to customize the testing environment.

Karma loads the files that have been included within the "files" array entry. Since this boilerplate is using Webpack and the module system, these files are loaded via a single script file: spec-bundle.js. This ensures that all the required dependencies of the project have been loaded successfully.

The "preprocessors" entry allows us to define a processing tool for each entry that has been defined in the "files" section. In our case, the files that have been loaded should be compiled using Webpack and its relevant Webpack test configuration file (the "webpack" entry is a custom entry key that is being read only by the karma-webpack plugin). In addition to that, multiple preprocessors can be run on each entry in our boilerplate. The "coverage" and "sourcemap" preprocessors are useful for creating a coverage summary for the test's results and a source map dictionary file for the typescript files of the application's code. The "coverage" preprocessors create a new directory with the results formatted as a mini HTML website (this is defined in the "coverageReporter" entry).

Karma-Supported Frameworks

Karma is agnostic for several values within the configuration file. It can run the tests on any browser that has had its launcher loaded as a plugin. Most browsers have a launcher. In addition to that, tests can be run on multiple browsers simultaneously. This is defined in the "browsers" entry.

Karma is also agnostic to the testing framework that is being used for writing and asserting tests. Each framework should be plugged into karma with a dedicated adapter. In our boilerplate, we are using Jasmine. It's also the default testing framework being used by the Angular team and is documented on the documentation website of Angular (`https://angular.io/docs/ts/latest/guide/`).

Configuring Karma's Output Results

In order to display the results of tests, karma uses the "reporters" entry to figure out who or what it should report the result to. A reporter is usually a script that sends the result to an output device. This output device can be the terminal, an HTML file, or a Continuous Integration (CI) server (i.e., Travis-ci, Jenkins). Karma includes the default reporters "dots" and "progress." Our boilerplate is configured to use the default reporter "mocha," which prints the description of each test (or, more precisely, a spec) in a green color with a success or error indicator (which will be then printed in a red color). In addition, the "coverage" reporter is used in conjunction with its preprocessor to output a coverage result for the whole application.

Karma's Test Process Modes

Two entries that are important to notice are "singleRun" and "autoWatch." The "singleRun" entry tells karma to run all the tests exactly once and then exit the process and terminate the test task. This is useful when the test process is integrated with a CI such as "Travis-CI" or "Jenkins". If this entry is set to `false`, then the process of the test runs the tests once and then hangs and waits for another command; the task is terminated. This usually goes along with the "autoWatch" entry, which tells karma to watch for changes within the files that have been loaded. If set to `true`, karma will run the tests again as long as the process is alive. It is disregarded when "singleRun" is set to `true`.

There are more settings that have been defined within the karma.conf.js file; however, we overviewed the important ones for our needs in this book. There is very good documentation on karma's website as well as other useful information. Table 2-1 summarizes the settings relevant to the karma.conf.js boilerplate that we'll work with in this book.

Table 2-1. *Summary of Karma Configuration File in This Book's Boilerplate*

Karma Entry	Plugins
Testing Framework	Jasmine
Preprocessors	Webpack, coverage, sourcemap
Browsers	Chrome
Single Run	true
Reporters	mocha, coverage

Webpack

Webpack is a module bundler tool, but it has lots more to offer. Webpack provides a very thorough toolset for bundling projects, running a development and testing environment, and much more.

As I stated before, there are four Webpack configuration files in our boilerplate. Each one includes the proper configuration settings for its purpose, be it development, production, testing, or Github deployment. However, there are common settings that all four share; these are configured in the webpack.common.js file.

Webpack Common Settings

Let's review the common settings in the webpack.common.js file. You'll notice first that there are a few required node modules that we'll use later as plugins for post-processing.

There are constants there that are used for the following:

1. **title** – defines the title that will be rendered in the index.html title element

2. **baseUrl** – used for defining index.html, the "base" URL element for loading related URLs

3. **isDevServer** – used by the Webpack Dev Server package in order to include the webpack-dev-server.js file in index.html

```
/*
 * Webpack Constants
 */
const HMR = helpers.hasProcessFlag('hot');
const METADATA = {
  title: 'Echoes Player Lite - Open Source Media Player for Youtube',
  baseUrl: '/',
  isDevServer: helpers.isWebpackDevServer()
};
```

■ **Note**   Webpack Dev Server is a complementary npm package separate from Webpack. It is a small web server based on nodejs and express.js, and is used to serve Webpack bundles during development only. For more info, go to https://webpack.github.io/docs/webpack-dev-server.html.

A Webpack configuration file eventually produces a json object. The boilerplate exports a function, which returns this configuration object. In the following sections, I will focus on some of these configuration options that represent the actual configuration that Webpack is using.

Entry

Via "Entry," we can define bundles that Webpack will start from; it eventually produces bundled files. This is a simple key-value object in which the key represents the name of the output file and the value represents the starting point for bundling the file and its dependencies.

The following three files are produced in our boilerplate:

1. polyfills – required libraries for adding missing functionality to old browsers (like es6 features and others)

2. vendor – third-party library files, such as Angular's packages, RxJS, ngrx's files, and others

3. main – the actual code of the application that we write on our own

```
entry: {

    'polyfills': './src/polyfills.browser.ts',
    'vendor':    './src/vendor.browser.ts',
    'main':      './src/main.browser.ts'

},
```

Resolve

"Resolve" is a group of settings that can be used to configure how files are resolved when required. Since we're going to use Typescript to write code and then load files with a .ts extension, this can be useful.

```
resolve: {

    /*
     * An array of extensions that should be used to resolve modules.
     *
     * See: http://webpack.github.io/docs/configuration.html#resolve-
         extensions
     */
    extensions: ['', '.ts', '.js', '.json'],

    // Make sure root is src
    root: helpers.root('src'),

    // remove other default values
    modulesDirectories: ['node_modules'],

},
```

Module: pre-loaders, loaders, and post-loaders

The "module" setting is one of the most useful settings and is an interesting option in Webpack. This setting is what makes Webpack a module loader that is agnostic to the extension of the module.

A loader, in Webpack's world, is a kind of plugin that assists Webpack in importing a file to the application and parsing it as it should be. A loader is defined using a simple json object. For example, in order to be able to load HTML files as strings, we can use raw-loader and define it like so:

```
{
        test: /\.html$/,
        loader: 'raw-loader',
        exclude: [helpers.root('src/index.html')]
}
```

This json object is added to the "loaders" array and provides the following instructions for Webpack:

1. test – a regular expression that applies this loader when one of the import or require statements points to a file with a .html extension

2. loader – Use one or more loaders to load this (html) type of file; in this case, use raw-loader only.

3. exclude (optional) – Ignore these paths/files before you try to load the file.

Now you can understand how Webpack can treat any kind of file as a module by using any type of loader.

■ **Note**   A loader is an npm package that can be installed with the npm command line. The convention for naming a loader is usually appending the word "loader" as a post-fix. There's no need to import the loader—Webpack does that.

The "pre-loaders" array is a collection of loaders that process the loaded files before the primary loaders are applied. The "post-loader" array is a collection of loaders that process the loaded files after the pre-loaders and loaders are applied.

There are several methods by which to apply multiple loaders to the same type of file.

1. Array of strings – each loader is defined separately and is applied by the order of the array; i.e., loaders: ['to-string-loader', 'css-loader']

2. Separated by "!" – each loader is separated by "!" in one string. Webpack applies the loaders from *right* to *left*; i.e., loaders: 'to-string-loader!css-loader'

Plugins

"Plugins" is a collection of processors that operates on the bundles after both the loading and its processors are complete. It's like post-processing the output result of Webpack's file bundling.

Webpack's object, "webpack," includes several built-in plugins. Usually, a plugin is the result of a newly created object, such as:

```
new webpack.optimize.CommonsChunkPlugin({
        name: ['polyfills', 'vendor'].reverse()
})
```

The order of the plugins in this array doesn't matter (unless plugins apply to the same bundle or for a common goal).

Similar to loaders, a plugin is usually a function that is applied by Webpack's compiler.

Node

The "Node" settings supply polyfills or mocks for various objects in the node environment.

Customized Settings

There are more settings with which to customize Webpack's build. Some of the settings that we're going to review in this section are configured with a different or additional value in each Webpack configuration file.

This is so we apply values that are proper for the intended goal. For instance, in a production bundle we would like to minify the bundle and perhaps use lite source maps, which should be loaded from an external source once needed. We might want to use special development settings, which can make the development workflow faster and may assist us in being more productive.

■ **Note** The webpack.common.js configuration is merged with any of the other Webpack configuration files at runtime. The other files add their settings to the common file and don't override it.

Output

The "Output" setting is the counterpart to "Entry." Contrary to the entry setting, there should only be one output setting; this affects all entries. Let's review some of the options in this setting. The output file's extension is a JavaScript (*.js) extension file.

- **filename** – We can set the name of the output file by using brackets. [name].bundle.js is an example of a technique used for template-like variables that should be applied to each entry (when multiple entries are configured).

- **path** – This is the target directory where the file should be placed at the end of compilation.

- **sourceMapFilename** – We can set the template name for the sourcemap file that is generated: [file].map.

For more options, navigate to `https://webpack.github.io/docs/configuration.html#output`.

devtool

This setting allows Webpack to create source maps to the generated files in various ways. A source map is a standard way to interpret transpiled code to its origin. This feature enables us to view the original source code as it is written (i.e., in Typescript) in the browser's developer tool.

Webpack's "devtool" setting enables few useful values. Each setting has its pros and cons in terms of build performance, rebuild performance, quality of the generated code, and production support. These configurations are shown in Table 2-2.

Table 2-2. *Summary of Webpack's Devtool Configuration Values (adapted from `https://webpack.github.io/docs/configuration.html#devtool`)*

Devtool value	Build Speed	Rebuild Speed	Production
eval	3	3	no
cheap-eval-source-map	1	2	no
cheap-source-map	1	0	yes
cheap-module-eval-source-map	0	2	no
cheap-module-source-map	0	-	yes
eval-source-map	-	1	no
source-map	-	-	yes

This concludes our introduction to Webpack and its responsibilities in our boilerplate.

Third-Party Libraries

Next, I will focus on the correct files that allow us to add third-party libraries. I call these "correct" since there is a reason for adding third-party libraries using these files.

As discussed in the Webpack section, there are three bundles of files—main.browser.ts, vendor.browser.ts, and polyfill.browser.ts—each of which includes portions of the code and libraries that we use for our application. For performance reasons, it is a best practice to include as few as possible outgoing requests within our index.html file so our application loads faster.

Since main.browesr.ts includes the code that we add to the application—the code that we write—we will focus on the other two main bundle files right now: vendor.browser.ts and polyfills.browser.ts. Lets understand each file's purpose and contents.

Vendor Libraries (vendor.browser.ts)

Located in the root of the src directory, vendor.browser.ts is the file that is compiled with Webpack's "vendor" entry. Here's an excerpt that shows the importing of Angular's two packages:

```
import '@angular/platform-browser';
import '@angular/platform-browser-dynamic';
import '@angular/core';
import '@angular/common';
import '@angular/forms';
import '@angular/http';
import '@angular/router';
```

In the following chapters, we will add third-party libraries like @ngrx/store, which will be included once and will be served from the output file vendor.js.

As of the time of writing this book, it is advised to include imports of specific RxJS operators and objects within this file in order to reduce the inclusion of redundant code in our applications.

You will notice that, thanks to Webpack's DefinePlugin plugin, there's a reference to a global "ENV" variable. DefinePlugin allows us to define global environment variables that we can use inside our application, treating it like a node.js environment. This is useful in case we would like to write code that should run only when our application is in production mode.

Polyfills (polyfills.browser.ts)

Polyfill in web development is a term coined by Remy Sharp (https://remysharp.com) back in 2010. A Polyfill is a code snippet (usually one file) that provides an implementation of a feature to compensate for the lack of this feature in browsers that don't support it yet. Here's an excerpt of the polyfills.browser.ts file importing some ES6 core implementations:

```
import 'core-js/es6/symbol';
import 'core-js/es6/object';
import 'core-js/es6/function';
import 'core-js/es6/parse-int';
```

```
import 'core-js/es6/parse-float';
import 'core-js/es6/number';
import 'core-js/es6/math';
```

As of the time of writing this book, only some of ES6 features are supported in most browsers. In order to use ES6 features in all browsers, we add implementations of these features in this file. Other non-related ES6 features should be included in this file as well. For instance, zone.js is included in this file as it's currently not part of any spec and has been proposed to the TC39 (Ecmascript Technical Committee).

The App Directory

The writing of components and logic is one of the most important takeaways of this book. Mostly, we'll focus on the app directory's contents in order to add new components, reducers, and services. Let's look at this directory.

App Component

In the root of the app directory, the main application's module is defined and its complementary files reside. I will review some of the most important files relevant to the project we are tackling in this book.

app.module.ts

This file is the main module. Eventually, Angular bootstraps it as the application in main. browser.ts. We will import other modules in this file and define them as needed. A good example of a module is the HttpModule.

app.component.ts

This is the main application component. Its template usually outlines the main structure of the application. It can include high-level components (container components) without any input properties. These high-level components can be feature modules.

In Echoes Player, the "app.component.ts" template includes some high-level components and one route outlet component to which a different component is rendered when the route changes.

Core Directory

The core directory includes a few core elements that are defined as the app's base elements that every module might use. The app/core directory includes the following directories inside:

- components
- directives
- services

23

- interfaces

- pipes

- store (with its reducers)

- effects (side effects with ngrx/effects)

In this book, we will focus on the core/store and core/effects directories when creating the core reactive elements that the app will use. Let's do a quick review of these directories.

The contents of the core directory are wrapped in a CoreModule, which is defined in index.ts. This is a shared module that every module can import and use its exported features.

Store Directory

This module defines the core store module that the app can use. The store incorporates ngrx/store as the reactive state-management solution.

Eventually, this directory will include directories of reducers and actions. Each directory defines a reducer for handling its state updates or actions that will be used as "tokens" to dispatch a state update.

"*.reducer.ts" File

A reducer is a pure function that takes both a new state and an action object as arguments and returns a new state based on the action's type and payload (optional relevant data that has been attached to this property).

A reducer is a portion of the store and represents a certain data structure in the store. It is a function that may transform the representation of a state and produce a new value to be saved within the store object. Usually, a reducer will be similar to the following structure:

```
// my-reducer.reducer.ts
import { ActionReducer, Action } from '@ngrx/store';
import { MyReducerActions } from './my-reducer.actions';

export interface SomeInterface {
    items: Item[],
    filter: string
}
let initialState: SomeInterface = {
    items: [],
    filter: ''
}
```

```
export functoin MyReducer (state:
SomeInterface = initialState, action: Action): ActionReducer<SomeInterface> {

    switch (action.type) {
        case MyReducerActions.ADD_ITEMS:
            return Object.assign({}, state, { items: [...items, ...action.
            payload] });

        case MyReducerActions.UPDATE_FILTER:
            return Object.assign({}, state, { filter: action.payload });

        default:
            return state;
    }
}
```

This is a common body structure for a reducer function. It includes a switch statement, which returns a new state object (or the same state) according to the action's type.

It's important to note that a reducer must return a *new* state object and not just mutate the state in any form. This is one of the characters of a pure function, and by returning a new state object, Angular can leverage the performance of state changes. It may boost performance of change detection by identifying which objects have changed, thus running the change cycle only when necessary and saving the browser from re-rendering components that don't need an update.

We'll dive into this in more detail in the following chapters.

Effects Directory

This directory includes various side effects that result from some of the actions that we'll work with. A *side effect* in this context is usually a "chain" of actions—a flow where a certain action should always followed by another action.

An effect is defined with the decorator @Effect:

```
// some-effect.effect.ts
@Effect()
addItemsReady$ = this.actions$
    .ofType(MyReducerActions.ADD_ITEMS)
    .map(action => action.payload)
    .switchMap(items => this.someServiceInfo.fetchMoreData(items)
      .map(items => this.myReducerActions.queueItems(items))
      .catch(() => Observable.of(this.myReducerActions.addItemsFailed(media)))
    );
```

This @Effect decorator reacts to the ADD_ITEMS action. Whenever this action is dispatched, there should be a side effect—a call to the fetchMoreData method, which results in new observable objects. This is why we use switchMap to "listen" to the new stream. When this stream is resolved, the second action object should be invoked by the myReducerActions action creator and handled by the MyReducer reducer. If something goes wrong, a good practice is to define a "catch" handler that dispatches an action object with addItemsFailed.

■ **Note**   An action creator is a function that takes one or more optional data arguments and returns an action object with both type and payload. This method encapsulates the attachment of the action type and provides a simple pure function with which to dispatch an action. This also makes code that uses an action creator easier to test and reason about.

Using a layer of effects is useful for several use cases. In this layer, we can initiate requests in order to update a backend service. It is also useful for updating or adding additional data to a state (think of paging lists of data). Beyond that, it promotes the perspective of designing services as "pure" stateless objects, allowing us to use it for fetching and updating data from/to a backend service while not keeping the state in these objects, but rather keeping it in our store.

We'll go into more depth with effects later in this book so we can understand how they contribute to the structure and flow of logic in our application (or any other application).

Services Directory

This directory includes the core services of this application. Usually, feature modules should consume these services in order to interact with external data API (YouTube's API, in this case).

Most of the code is already written for these services; however, we'll update these as we go along with the book in order to experiment and understand reactive programming with services in Angular.

Other Directories (home)

In this level of directories, next to the app.*.ts files, we'll create container components (smart components) for those components that have access to the application's services and core features.

The HomeModule includes the home component, which is an example of such a container component. It stands on its own and connects to the store and services of the application.

We'll create several smart components, each of which will eventually be activated via routes that we'll create. Each smart component may define its own nested routes to which other components are attached.

To create modular and maintainable components, it is very useful to create smaller, nested components within the smart component directory (not necessarily attached to nested routes).

Running the Project

Let's go ahead and run this chapter's code. After you have downloaded this chapter's project files from the chapter-02 directory, open a terminal (or a command line). There are a few preliminary steps to take to prepare our project to run.

1. run npm install (or npm i as a shortcut). This will install all the required dependencies of this project. This takes some time, but no more than two or three minutes (depending on your Internet connection).

2. run npm start. This will compile the project and run a local server.

Once you see these lines in the terminal (Figure 2-2), it means that the compile phase has been completed successfully and that you can navigate to the browser to see the project.

```
webpack: bundle is now VALID.
[default] Checking started in a separate process...
[default] Ok, 2.103 sec.
```

Figure 2-2. Lines indicating that the compiling phase has been completed

Now you can open the browser and navigate to http://localhost:3000. You should be able to see an empty application skeleton (Figure 2-3), which we'll add components to in the next chapters.

Figure 2-3. Empty boilerplate awaiting use

Alternative Boilerplates

The AngularClass boilerplate is just one of a few boilerplates that you can start an Angular-based application with. There are many other boilerplates with additional features and concepts, such as the following:

- Server-side rendering

- Angular material

- ES6-only boilerplate

- Other UI libraries

The Official Angular CLI Tool

At the time of writing this book, the Angular team has released the first official version—1.0.0—of the angular-cli tool for creating Angular-based applications. It is an open source project available at https://github.com/angular/angular-cli.

This tool is a command-line interface for creating new Angular applications and generating code during development. With a few short, simple commands in the command line, you can create new components, services, and other common files.

The main command you would use to interact with this tool in the command line is ng. The angular-cli tool abstracts the use of Webpack and karma, as well as a lot of the configurations and tools that have been covered in this chapter. The store and effects files are not part of this tool yet. In addition, it includes several npm scripts for running various tasks for testing, building, and production.

Summary

In this chapter I introduced the boilerplate code that the Echoes Player (Lite) application will be based on. We reviewed the main build tool, which orchestrates all files in order to assist us with many useful operations, such as writing Typescript and compiling it to a one-bundle JavaScript file.

I also introduced the directories and file structure of this boilerplate, pointing to the important directories where we will add ngrx/store and ngrx/effects.

In the next chapter, we will dive into state management with the ngrx/store library and will connect it to a component.

CHAPTER 3

■ ■ ■

Adding State Management with ngrx/store

One of the most important aspects of software development is state management. With each development project, there's some sort of tracking being done of data over time as well as of any updates made to that data.

When approaching the user interface in front-end development, it's important to have a single source of truth when it comes to data. The UI should display the exact state of data. In JavaScript, it is very easy to lose a reference to a data structure, thus creating ghost references that can cause a false presentation of the wrong data.

With Angular version 1, one of the common best practices for keeping and tracking state was to manage it in services (and not in controllers). However, even then, the implementation of how to update this state completely relied on the developer. Tracking the state updates and predicating it was eventually a difficult task. There had to be something better.

In this chapter, we'll discuss the benefits of state management and how it leverages consistent, predictable state changes. We'll start to dive in to Angular's ngrx suite with the ngrx/store library as well as RxJS-based state management. We will integrate ngrx/store into our application, connecting the state to components and eventually displaying it on screen.

Benefits of Store as State Management

ngrx/store is a library for state management for Angular applications. Before we start to understand the technical details of ngrx/store, it's important to understand the advantages of integrating a store solution and how it contributes to development, production, and testing phases.

One Place for State

A store solution dictates keeping the state of the application in one directory. This makes it easier to predict updates or changes to the state's structure and how it is manipulated and stored before it is saved by the reducer.

© Oren Farhi 2017
O. Farhi, *Reactive Programming with Angular and ngrx*,
DOI 10.1007/978-1-4842-2620-9_3

Performance

Utilizing unidirectional flow, relying on individual state changes while taking advantage of observables, makes Angular's change detection more precise and performant, as it is intended to make use of the marking of direct paths in need of updating.

Testability

Since the store is a collection of reducers—pure functions—it is easy to write tests for such functions; given the same inputs, pure functions should output the same results. Moreover, pure functions don't produce side effects; i.e., changing or updating variables outside its scope. Each test may cover a wide variety of cases, which a coverage report may sum up at the end.

Devtools

All of the preceding elements lead to a very productive base for creating helpful developer tools that can assist you when developing with a store solution. Redux (which was introduced in chapter 1) was first introduced with the concept of "time traveling"— watching the state as it changes and being able to control it and understand how, when, and why things go wrong while developing. Other useful features are available by connecting to the store before and after actions are dispatched—both client and backend storage, logging (client and backend), and any other "middleware" that can offer a useful feature.

Redux Primer

As I mentioned earlier, state management in front-end applications comes in many forms. Simply put, "state management" refers to simple CRUD (Create, Read, Update, and Delete) actions: retrieving state, changing state, deleting a state, as well as creating a new state.

Redux has answers for many of the challenges of how to achieve correct state management. Redux is a predictable state-management solution for applications. Developed by Dan Abramov, Redux is a library that implements the ideas of Flux. Flux is a design pattern that popularized one-way data flow (a.k.a. unidirectional flow), which was first presented by Facebook.

Flux

In the core of the Flux pattern, the flow for performing CRUD actions should be in one direction. The state should be updated by dispatching an action to the store and not by directly manipulating it. Once the store is updated, the view should re-render the latest state.

There have been dozens of implementations for Flux. Some of them used a more thorough way of handling multiple stores and actions, while some took a simpler approach. Redux took the simpler approach, eventually gaining popularity in state management for front-end applications.

ngrx/store is an implementation of Redux that was developed with RxJS while keeping the core concepts and API of Redux. Before we dive into ngrx/store, we'll review the basic concepts of Redux.

Redux in Action

Redux is a JavaScript library for state management. Although it was developed around the React framework, it's agnostic to any framework. Taking ideas from Flux and Elm, it helps you design an application with consistent behavior while leveraging the power of functional programming.

In Redux, the state is kept in a store. A store is essentially a singleton object that is a reference to some structure of data. This data is updated via pure functions, which are called *reducers*. The return value of a reducers creates a *new state* in the store. In the following code snippet, we create a simple reducer function that returns a value to indicate whether a light switch is switched on or off:

```
import { createStore } from 'redux';

// reducer
function lightSwitch(state = 0, action) {
  switch (action.type) {
    case 'LIGHT_ON':
      return 1;
    case 'LIGHT_OFF':
      return 0;
    default:
      return state;
  }
}
```

To connect this reducer to the store, we use the createStore function:

```
let store = createStore(lightSwitch);
```

In order to switch the light on and off, we start dispatching the appropriate actions:

```
store.dispatch({ type: 'LIGHT_ON' }); // switch the light on - '1'
store.dispatch({ type: 'LIGHT_OFF' }); // switch the light off - '0'
```

In order to listen to events whenever a value changes in the store, we can subscribe to the store:

```
store.subscribe( () => {
  console.log(store.getState()); // outputs the state
});
```

These are the basics of using Redux as a state-management solution with any framework. However, Redux has gone beyond this and includes much more. It includes middleware that allows extensibility to the library while connecting plugins; i.e., adding asynchronous actions to mutate the state.

Reduce and Flux for Redux

Considering that the state is kept in an array while reducers are used for manipulating the actual data in the Flux store, to implement the store, the reduce function (from the array) takes another function as the first parameter and an initial value as the second parameter. Finally, the output of a reduce operation contains one value.

The concept of having a reduce function for each slice of the state fits nicely into the Array.reduce function, utilizing both performance in producing a new state (array) and boilerplate code in applying a state change once an action is called.

ngrx/store

ngrx/store is essentially Redux for Angular. Underneath, it is based on RxJS and implements the Redux API while exposing the nature of the RxJS API. This gives asynchronous support from the start to the store, since RxJS unifies both synchronous and asynchronous event handling.

Similar to Redux, ngrx/store is based on unidirectional flow, as shown in Figure 3-1.

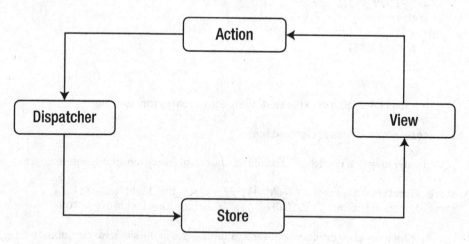

Figure 3-1. *Simple ngrx/store state flow*

Next, we'll dive into ngrx/store and its implementation while integrating it into our application.

Core Concepts

Similar to Redux, use of ngrx/store is designed around three main objects:

1. store
2. reducers
3. actions

Underneath the hood, there are even more objects, which makes working with these three a breeze.

Store

A store is a singleton object that holds the state of the application. It should be regarded as *the one and only single* source of data that is delivered to the application. By following this rule, the store represents the application's true and only state at any time.

The store can be thought of as an object with an Event Bus' features, among others. Because one of its main goals is to keep and track a state, in order to be notified of a state update, we can "subscribe" to the store. On the other hand, to change the state, we can "dispatch" an action with a new state value.

To achieve that, the store includes two important features of RxJS: an *observable* and an *observer*.

Rx.Observable

An observable is an object that holds data that might be updated over time. It can be subscribed to in order to get notifications when something has been updated or changed. In other words, this object allows the store to save and track data, to be "observed" by its subscribers, and be notified once there is a change.

It's important to distinguish between two types of observables. A "hot" observable produces values even before it has been subscribed to (i.e., mouse move events). A "cold" observable produces values only after it has been subscribed to by an observer.

This is a simple observable that emits the values 1, 2, and 3 and then completes the process.

```
var observable = Rx.Observable.create(observer => {
    observer.next(1);
    observer.next(2);
    observer.next(3);
    observer.complete();
});
```

Often, the data that is sent out through the observable is referred to as a *stream*. Although it seems to be simple, before the observable emits the values of the stream to its subscribers (in the case of cold observables, once subscribed to), these values can be transformed by operator functions. Much like in JavaScript arrays, for example, the values can be mapped to new values before they are sent to the subscribed functions:

```
var observable = Rx.Observable.create(observer => {
  observer.next(1);
  observer.next(2);
  observer.next(3);
  observer.complete();
}).map(value => value * 2);
```

Rx.Observer

An observer is an object that can subscribe to an observable object. In other words, this object allows the store to watch for updates in its state and then lets this update move on to the next subscribers.

An observer should implement at least one function out of three that an observable might call over time: next(x), error(e), and complete(). To connect an observer to an observable and start receiving values, the subscribe method should be used:

```
var observable = Rx.Observable.create(observer => {
    observer.next(1);
    observer.next(2);
    observer.next(3);
    observer.complete();
});

var observer = {
  next: (value) => console.log(value),
  error: (err) => console.log(err),
  complete: () => console.log('done!')
};
observable.subscribe(observer);
```

■ **Note**   Only after subscribing to an observable can the values be emitted. Each subscribe method creates a new execution for the subscribed function.

An observable can have multiple observers subscribed to it. However, since RxJS creates a new execution for each subscriber, if values are transformed (i.e., with map), each subscriber will get the most recent transformed values.

```
var observable = Rx.Observable.create(observer => {
  observer.next(1);
  observer.next(2);
  observer.next(3);
  observer.complete();
}).map(value => value * 2);
```

```
observable.subscribe(val => console.log('1st', val));
observable.subscribe(val => console.log('2nd', val * 2));
```

The output for this code would be:

```
1st 2
1st 4
1st 6
2nd 4
2nd 8
2nd 12
```

However, looking back at the store concept in Redux, we would like the data to be both observable and an observer. On the one hand, we would like to observe the store's data for any changes. On the other hand, we would like to perform some operations on this data before emitting these values to potential subscribers.

Rx.BehaviorSubject

A BehaviorSubject is a composition of an observable object and an observer object. This can really be thought of as a special Event Bus (or Event Emitter) that tracks its data and emits the current value once it is subscribed to. It stores the latest emitted value, which is delivered to any subscriber once it subscribes.

Because of this special feature of storing the latest emitted value, the BehaviorSubject is a perfect match for store-related implementation. It reduces boilerplate code with its observable and observer natures as well as tracks and stores data for later use.

■ **Note** A BehaviorSubject is a variant of Rx.Subject, which is a fundamental composition of observable and observer that is used for other variants of Subject as well.

A few of the main objects in ngrx/store are based on BehaviorSubject: dispatcher, reducer, and state. Each of these extends BehaviorSubject and makes use of both its observable and observer natures for emitting values next to the main store stream.

Reducers

A reducer is a pure function (of type ActionReducer). It expects two values as input arguments: the previous state and an action object, which includes an action type and an optional payload property. It should output a new state object as a return value. For that reason, it is easy to test reducers and potentially cover all the relevant cases this function should handle.

The store is composed of one or several reducers, so each reducer represents a portion of data and a way to change it in the store. It follows the reducer pattern of Redux.

For each reducer, an instance of the Reducer class is created, which is based on a BehaviorSubject. It leverages the observable and observer advantages and emits the updated state to the store's stream.

An important rule to keep in mind regarding reducers is that it should always return a new state object and *not* mutate it directly. The newly updated state is then delivered to the relevant subscribe method, so you shouldn't worry about losing a reference to the state object where it is consumed.

A reducer operates on the arguments it receives. The first argument, the previous state, is usually used to construct a new state, copying data that should not change. Meanwhile, the data sent as the second argument, action, dictates what data should change in the state. Usually, a reducer function body would be similar to this:

```
export function user (state = {}, action: Action): ActionReducer<IUser> {
  switch (action.type) {
    case "UPDATE_NAME":
    return Object.assign({}, state, { name: action.payload });
    case "LOG_OUT":
    return Object.assign({}, {
      logged_in: false,
      name: ''
    });
    default:
    return state;
  }
}
```

Action

To update the state, an action should be emitted. An action object as received in the reducer function is composed of a *type* and a *payload* (optional). The type is a string value that is evaluated with a switch statement.

The payload property is optional and may include any data type. If the action should carry any relevant data that should update the state, then the payload will hold this data.

Emitting an action is performed using the store's dispatch method. It's the only way to update the state in the store; no other way should be used instead. Once an action is dispatched, the store performs a reduce process with all its registered reducers, produces a new state, and updates subscribers.

A common practice that we will use is creating an action using *action creators*. Action creators receive one optional argument as payload data and return an object with the action type and payload. Since the emitting of actions is common, we can reuse an action object creation, encapsulating its creation and ensuring the exact action type is attached to the returned object. This also allows us to use a mockup for tests that require these actions.

As an example for defining an *"action creator"*, if want to dispatch an action for updating a user name, we can just call the `updateName` method (considering it exists and has been imported by a service or on its own) and pass it as an argument to `dispatch`:

```
updateName(name: string): Action {
    return {
      type: "UPDATE_NAME",
      payload: name
    };
}
// usage
this.store.dispatch(updateName("oren"))
```

This sums up the core concepts of ngrx/store. Next, we're going to connect it to our application, add our first reducer, and display it on screen.

Adding ngrx/store

Now that we understand the basic concepts of ngrx/store, it is time to actually connect it to our application within the relevant files and start using it as a state-management tool. To do so, we need to perform these main steps, all of which are detailed in the following sections.

1. Install npm packages.

2. Define the main store module.

3. Create YouTube Videos reducer.

4. Connect the reducer to the store.

5. Connect the reducer to a component.

Installing NPM Packages

ngrx/store can be installed via an npm registry as an npm package. It is divided into ngrx/core and ngrx/store. To install, we can simply use npm:

```
npm install ngrx/store ngrx/core --save-dev
```

Defining the Main Store Module

`Files` This section refers to the src/app/core/store directory.

ngrx/store is an Angular module; however, we'll define our application store's module such that we can simply include it in the main application module. There is no need for a separate module.

Let's focus on the index.ts file in this directory. First, we import all the objects relevant for creating a store:

```
import { NgModule } from '@angular/core';
import { Store, StoreModule } from '@ngrx/store';

import { ActionReducer, Action, combineReducers } from '@ngrx/store';
import { compose } from '@ngrx/core/compose';
```

Next, we define placeholders. Currently these will be empty, but rest assured—we will add the relevant code later. We then define an interface for the store EchoesState. This will assist us in development, providing code-completion and error-reporting assistance. With that, we define an actions array that is provided to our module so we can later import actions from files.

Finally, we include the reducers object, which holds function reducer references and will be used to create the store object that holds the app's data.

```
export interface EchoesState {

}

const actions = [

];

const reducers = { };
```

Next, we define our own CoreStoreModule, ready to be imported to our main application module file.

```
@NgModule({
  imports: [
    StoreModule.provideStore(composeStore),
  ],
  declarations: [

  ],
  exports: [

  ],
  providers: [ ...actions ]
})
export class CoreStoreModule {};
```

Actually, this module is already connected to the application's main module through the core module (src/app/core/index.ts). This means that the store object is available to any other module that consumes the application's core module.

Currently, there's nothing in the store to consume and show on the screen. Let's create our first reducer.

Creating a YouTube Videos Reducer

Files This section refers to the src/app/core/store/youtube-videos directory.

The YouTube videos reducer is responsible for storing an array of YouTube media item objects. This directory includes four files:

youtube-videos/index.ts

This file exports this reducer's actions and reducer function so it can be easily connected to the store once imported.

```
export * from './youtube-videos.reducer';
export * from './youtube-videos.actions';
```

youtube-videos/youtube-videos.actions.ts

In this file, we declare the actions that this reducer can handle as well as the actions that are allowed to be dispatched by the application's modules.

The actions are available via a service that can be consumed by any module of the app (Injectable). However, we're going to use action creators to encapsulate its creation and reuse. Notice that each action is defined as a static property with a prefix. This ensures the uniqueness of each action once reducers are invoked. The Action interface is imported so as to hint at the return value for each action creator function.

```
import { Injectable } from '@angular/core';
import { Action } from '@ngrx/store';

@Injectable()
export class YoutubeVideosActions {
  static ADD = '[YoutubeVideos] ADD_VIDEOS';
  static RESET = '[YoutubeVideos] RESET';

  addVideo(videos: GoogleApiYouTubeVideoResource[]): Action {
    return {
      type: YoutubeVideosActions.ADD,
      payload: videos
    };
  }
  reset(): Action {
    return {
      type: YoutubeVideosActions.RESET
    };
  }
}
```

41

youtube-videos/youtube-videos.reducer.ts

The reducer file defines the function reducer that the store will run each time an action is dispatched.

First, the `ActionReducer` and `Action` interfaces are imported to make note of the reducer function type and its return value type.

Second, the interface `EchoesVideos` is defined for this reducer—an array that contains objects of type `GoogleApiYouTubeVideoResource`. We will use this interface when we connect the reducer to the store and also later on when we consume this reducer in presentation components. Again, this allows the Typescript linting as well as Typescript-aware code editors to assist with code completion and error reporting.

The `videos` `ActionReducer` is the actual reducer function. It expects a `state` array as a first argument, and if it's not present, it will initialize it to an empty array. It also expects an `action` object, which is handled by its type property and optionally by its `payload` property. Notice how the `RESET` case returns an empty array, so it doesn't need to use the action's payload.

```
import { ActionReducer, Action } from '@ngrx/store';
import { YoutubeVideosActions } from './youtube-videos.actions';

export interface EchoesVideos extends Array<GoogleApiYouTubeVideoResource> {};

export function videos (state: EchoesVideos =
[], action: Action): ActionReducer<EchoesVideos> {

  switch (action.type) {
    case YoutubeVideosActions.ADD:
      return [...state, ...action.payload];

    case YoutubeVideosActions.RESET:
      return [];

    default:
      return state;
  }
};
```

youtube-videos/youtube-videos.spec.ts

This file includes tests for the reducer. Since we're testing a simple JavaScript function, the tests are quite simple, and there's no need to connect it to Angular. Angular's default testing framework is called Jasmine. However, Angular is completely agnostic to the testing framework, and you are free to choose the proper solution as you see fit.

First, we need to import the `videos` function reducer and the relevant actions class. Next, we import a json object from a static file, which will be used as payload data for the ADD action. There are various ways in which we can add videos to the store. The most common way in the Echoes Player (Lite) is by searching YouTube with its data API.

However, we don't actually want to perform an ajax request to YouTube's API each time we test. Rather, we want to test the operation of adding videos to the store, especially whether the ajax request has successfully returned the response. For this reason, we import a json file, which is a mocked array of items from the tests directory (located in the root of the application).

```
import { videos } from './youtube-videos.reducer';
import { YoutubeVideosActions } from './youtube-videos.actions';
import { YoutubeMediaItemsMock } from '../../../../../tests/mocks/youtube.
        media.items';
```

Now, we are ready to create a test suite by using describe. Since the YoutubeVideosActions class doesn't store data or have any side effects, we can simply instantiate it once for the whole suite. Angular does this behind the scenes once this class is injected into our application. We have to do this manually here in order to gain access to its functions.

```
describe('The Youtube Videos reducer', () => {
  const mockedState = [];
  const youtubeVideosActions = new YoutubeVideosActions();
```

Next, there are three specs defined with the it function. Each spec should define its own expectation. For the first spec, I want make sure that the videos reducer function will return the same state if is given an action type that it does not handle. To test it, I simply run the function and send to it the state as the first argument and an action object with unknown type as the second. Then, I set the expectation to match the state.

```
it('should return current state when no valid actions have been made', () => {
  const state = [...mockedState];
  const actual = videos(state, { type: 'INVALID_ACTION', payload: {} });
  const expected = state;
  expect(actual).toBe(expected);
});
```

For the second spec, I want to test the ADD action. To do so, I call the videos function again. This time, the function receives as its second argument a mocked array of YouTube item objects while using the addVideos action creator to create a proper ADD action. Finally, I expect the state to change and include the new array in addition to what it had before.

```
it('should ADD videos', () => {
  const state = [...mockedState];
  const actual = videos(state, youtubeVideosActions.addVideos(YoutubeMediaI
                temsMock));
  const expected = [...state, ...YoutubeMediaItemsMock];
  expect(actual.length).toBe(expected.length);
});
```

For the last spec, I test the RESET action. For starters, I create an initial state object that includes the array of YouTube objects from the YoutubeMediaItemsMock file. Then, I call the videos reducer function with this initial state as the first argument (remember: this argument functions as the *current* state that exists in the store) while passing the reset() function (or action creator). As a result of calling this action, I expect the initial state to be empty, meaning its length should be equal to zero.

```
it('should empty the state when RESET', () => {
  const state = [...YoutubeMediaItemsMock];
  const actual = videos(state, youtubeVideosActions.reset());
  const expected = 0;
  expect(actual.length).toEqual(expected);
});
});
```

If we run the npm test in the terminal, crossing our fingers, we'll receive the test results (considering the tests in app.spec.ts are disabled with xdescribe since none will currently pass as the code for them has not been added yet) shown in Figure 3-2.

```
● ● ● 1. farhioren@Farhis-MacBook-Pro: ~/Projects/Clients/echoes-ng2-lite (zsh)
×  ..hoes-ng2-lite (zsh)  ⌘1
06 11 2016 13:48:30.949:INFO [launcher]: Starting browser Chrome
06 11 2016 13:48:31.913:INFO [Chrome 54.0.2840 (Mac OS X 10.12.0)]: Connected on so
cket /#9CVeT5S7X942L-6pAAAA with id 80883272
  App
    ✔ should be defined (skipped)
    ✔ should have 3 public services (skipped)
    ✔ should select a video in playlist (skipped)
  The Youtube Videos reducer
    ✔ should return current state when no valid actions have been made
    ✔ should ADD videos
    ✔ should empty the state when RESET
    ✔ should replace add new 50 objects when updating data when state is empty
    ✔ should replace 50 objects when updating data when state is not empty

Finished in 0.011 secs / 0.003 secs

SUMMARY:
✔ 5 tests completed
ⓘ 3 tests skipped

=============================== Coverage summary ===============================
Statements   : 45.24% ( 171/378 )
Branches     : 41.21% ( 68/165 )
Functions    : 14.42% ( 15/104 )
Lines        : 45.9% ( 168/366 )
================================================================================
```

Figure 3-2. Test results for the YouTube videos reducer

It is nice to see that all five of the specs of the YouTube videos reducer are marked with a green check mark (there are two more specs you can find within the source code).

With these results, we can rest assured that our reducer function will handle the data as we expect it to. It's important to realize that it's our responsibility to figure out and implement specs for all the edge cases that this reducer should handle.

Now that we have a reducer that is fully working and tested, it's time to connect the reducer to the store and connect the store to the application so as to view and display its contents.

Connecting Reducer to the Store

Files This section refers to the src/app/core/store/index.ts file.

To connect the YouTube videos reducer to the store, we need to import both the reducer function and its relevant actions class.

First, we import the videos reducer function and the YoutubeVideosActions class.

```
import { NgModule } from '@angular/core';
import { Store, StoreModule } from '@ngrx/store';
import { ActionReducer, Action, combineReducers } from '@ngrx/store';
import { compose } from '@ngrx/core/compose';

// reducers
import { videos, YoutubeVideosActions, EchoesVideos } from './youtube-videos';
```

We also import EchoesVideos in order to use it in the main store for defining the videos entry of type EchoesVideos. The YoutubeVideosActions class is added to the actions array, which is included later in this file as part of this module's "providers."

```
export interface EchoesState {
  videos: EchoesVideos;
}
const actions = [
  YoutubeVideosActions
];
```

We haven't connected the reducer yet. To make it officially connected to the main store, we simply have to add it as a key to the reducers object. This object is handed to the provideStore method, which creates the actual store instance.

```
const reducers = { videos };

@NgModule({
  imports: [
    StoreModule.provideStore(reducers),
  ],
  declarations: [
```

```
  ],
  exports: [

  ],
  providers: [ ...actions ]
})
export class CoreStoreModule {};
```

Now that the reducers are connected to our app, they are ready to be consumed in our components.

Connecting Reducer to a Component

Files This section refers to the src/app/youtube-videos/youtube-videos.component.ts file.

First, we need to import the store's objects that we'll work with in this component. We'll need the EchoesState interface, EchoesVideos interface, YoutubeVideosActions class, and YoutubeMediaItemsMock file (for demo purposes).

```
import { Component, EventEmitter, Input, Output, ChangeDetectionStrategy,
OnInit } from '@angular/core';
import { Observable } from 'rxjs/Observable';
import { Store } from '@ngrx/store';
import { EchoesState } from '../core/store';
import { EchoesVideos, YoutubeVideosActions } from '../core/store/youtube-videos';
import { YoutubeMediaItemsMock } from '../../../tests/mocks/youtube.media.items';
```

Next, we define a videos$ property on the YoutubeVideos component that will store a reference to the store's videos key. To make it Typescript-friendly, the EchoesVideos interface is used here to annotate that we're expecting an observable of the EchoesVideos type. Next, we inject the YoutubeVideosActions class and the Store objects into the constructor method. We use EchoesState in order to define a store of this type.

```
export class YoutubeVideosComponent implements OnInit {
  videos$: Observable<EchoesVideos>;

  constructor(
    private youtubeVideosActions: YoutubeVideosActions,
    private store: Store<EchoesState>
  ) {
  }
```

Now, we need to connect the videos$ property so it will "listen" to changes within the videos reducer in our store, so that each time this reducer is updated with a new state, this videos$ property is notified. The store's "select" method is used in order to define which slice of the state should be returned when the state changes. In this case, the "state.videos" is selected and returned to the observable member "videos$". It's better to connect this on the ngOnInit component lifecycle after any input parameters have been initialized.

```
ngOnInit() {
    this.videos$ = this.store.select(state => state.videos);

  this.store.dispatch(this.youtubeVideosActions.addVideos(YoutubeMediaItemsMock));
  }
```

Notice that for the sake of this demo, I dispatch the YoutubeMediaItemsMock array to mock a response of search results in YouTube. See how I use the youtubVideosActions in order to add videos to the reducer. This dispatch action will eventually invoke the videos reducer function and update the state using the ADD case.

The one last step—but still an important step for displaying something on the screen—is rendering the data from the videos$ observer using this component's template.

To use an observable in a view, we need to use the async pipe. Since videos$ is not an actual array, the async pipe enables us to extract the actual data from this object and use it in the view. (This is just a very brief introduction for the next chapter.) We use the async pipe to extract the data whenever it is changed in the videos$ observer, which is dependent on the videos reducer. Then, we render the length of this videos array.

```
@Component({
  selector: 'youtube-videos',
  template: `
  <article class="col-md-12">
    <h1>Search Results</h1>
    <code>
      There are {{ (videos$ | async).length }} videos
    </code>
  </article>
  `
})
```

There are several operations within this expression, as follows:

1. We ask the view to listen to the videos$ observer for changes.

2. After changes have happened, they are propagated into the html code of this component. We ask to evaluate the length property of the videos data object. This operation happens only after the data from the videos$ reducer has been resolved.

Now, we can run the application and see something:

1. Run this in the terminal: npm start.

2. Open the browser and navigate to http://localhost:3000.

You should be able to see something similar to what is shown in Figure 3-3, indicating the number of videos that exist in the videos reducer:

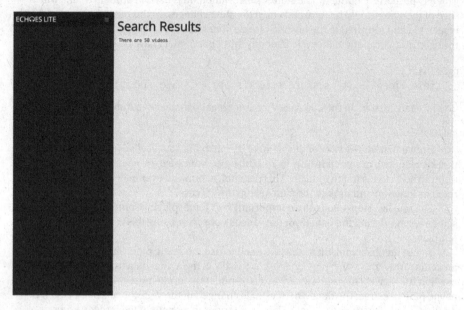

Figure 3-3. Rendering data from the videos reducer

We can take this further and render a list of videos with images:

```
@Component({
  selector: 'youtube-videos',
  template: `
  <article class="col-md-12">
    <h1>Search Results</h1>
    <code>
      There are {{ (videos$ | async).length }} videos
    </code>
    <ul class="list-unstyled">
      <li *ngFor="let video of (videos$ | async)">
        <img [src]="video.snippet.thumbnails.default.url">
        {{ video.snippet.title }}
      </li>
    </ul>
  </article>
  `
})
```

Figure 3-4. Rendering a list of videos from the videos reducer

Congratulations! You've just connected your real first reducer to the application's view.

Summary

In this chapter, I introduced the state-management concept and its popularity in JavaScript with Redux. I introduced ngrx/store as an RxJS-based state-management solution for Angular, along with its benefits and core concepts. Finally, I went through the required steps for adding ngrx/store to our application, creating the first reducer for the store, and consuming it in the view with a component.

In the following chapters, we will built on top of these concepts with more aspects of the application while incorporating additional reducers and techniques to work with it.

CHAPTER 4

■ ■ ■

Creating Reactive Components: Presentational and Container

Accompanied Code This chapter's boilerplate code is found in the chapter-04 file.

The Components approach to development has become quite popular, with several frameworks embracing its concept. Actually, the notion was conceived and used in JavaScript web development long before Angular, React, and other MV* frameworks were released. Some used the term *widget* while some used *plugins*.

With AngularJS (first version of Angular), the directive API was the standard method for creating custom HTML elements, better known as components. These components can be used in other components' templates throughout the application.

With the release of React and its focus on the View layer in web development, the Components Architecture approach gained even more traction and popularity.

Angular continued to embrace the nature of component-based architecture, leveraging the concept's advantages into a high-performance View layer while applying composition. Integrating reactive programming with components is an important concept when developing in Angular.

In this chapter, we will create several components for the Echoes Player (Lite) application. We will start by refreshing our memories about what smart and dumb components are. This will be followed by creating the now-playing smart component along with its presentational components: now-playlist and now-playlist-filter.

If you open the project (the chapter-04 file) in the browser, you should see something similar to what is shown in Figure 4-1. Providing any search term and hitting the Enter key will render relevant YouTube media results to the screen.

© Oren Farhi 2017
O. Farhi, *Reactive Programming with Angular and ngrx*,
DOI 10.1007/978-1-4842-2620-9_4

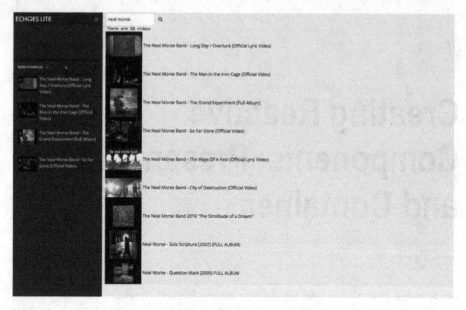

Figure 4-1. The Echoes project with a now-playing component

The now-playing smart component can be spotted on the left-hand gray sidebar. A media track is rendered once a thumbnail is clicked within the right area. It's completely reactive, an integration of the data coming from ngrx/store with the components that we will review within this chapter. While creating these components, we will go over several key concepts to follow when creating components in Angular, as follows:

1. Using the async pipe component's template (usually in the container component)

2. Integrating reactive programming with ngrx/store to create components

3. Using action creators for simpler store interactions as a "store-agnostic" way for components to interact with the store, doing so by using the `functions` interface rather than the hardcoded `store.dispatch` call.

Introduction to Components

By now, you might have seen or used components in some form. In the context of web development, a component is a reusable module. It should be able to function on its own (excluding its dependencies).

A component may get some parameters from the outside world in order to be displayed or to do some calculations with them. It may expose events, indicating that something has happened or changed in the component's internal sandbox.

A component must have a custom HTML tag associated with it so it can be used in the application. Usually, it also includes a template, which it operates on while encapsulating it with its tag.

HTML Components

Components were around even before the release of Angular. For example, if you have worked with HTML or JavaScript, you might have seen the following:

1. select component – a dropdown component

2. video component – a load and play video files component

Both of these HTML elements can be regarded as components because they contain the following characteristics:

1. Can be reused by a specific HTML tag

2. Include "input" parameters with attributes (src for video, selected for select)

3. Expose events when something has happened or changed within ("change" event for select, several media events for video)

4. Both encapsulate a sandboxed presentational template

In this chapter, we will create and review custom components for the now-playlist feature. Since it is similar to how the select and video components are structured, we will follow their building blocks and concepts. First, let's review these concepts.

The main concern for each of these components, select and video, is how they present data and when they should notification of events that something has happened or changed inside (events). These components have no control over the data they present. Both rely on external input, which is delivered through attributes. Moreover, in order to provide notification of events, JavaScript function callbacks are registered via the standard event listener API.

However, with these things in mind, let's look at the several unique features of each of these components that allow each to function. The video element encapsulates its inner components—the controls and the screen. It includes some internal implementation (which is delegated to the browser eventually) on how to load the source video file. It allows supporting internal components, source and track, which the internal implementation knows how and where to use.

However, in the world of JavaScript, we can make our own components and attach the logic we see fit for them to fill their purpose. At the end of the previous chapter, we created the custom component called youtube-videos. This kind of component doesn't expose any events or attributes that can be used outside; it contains internal logic that is responsible for fetching the data that it should display.

This is known as a container or a smart component. Let's review it now.

Container / Smart Component

A container component is concerned with how its internal operations work within its own sandbox boundaries. The now-playlist component is an example of a container component—it stands on its own and is responsible for connecting the now-playlist state with its internal components. It is also responsible for handling the events of the internal components and then dispatching the correct actions back to the store.

To summarize, a container component is smart enough to perform a few operations and make some decisions:

1. It is often responsible for fetching data that might be displayed.

2. It might be composed of several other components.

3. It is "stateful"—may manage a certain state.

4. It handles the internal components' events and async operations.

Let's walk through these characteristics and analyze how they are used in smart components.

Files This section refers to the src/app/youtube-videos/youtube-videos. component.ts file.

Fetching Data

At the end of the previous chapter, we used a mocked json file to add a collection of media files to the application's store. However, this was just for demo purposes. Since the youtube-videos component is a container component that is rendered via a route configuration, it is responsible for fetching the data it needs to display.

■ **Note** Data can also be fetched before a container component is rendered with a router "resolve" strategy.

Let's make the youtube-videos component more interactive. We will add a search box via which the user can search for any term.

```
@Component({
  selector: 'youtube-videos',
  template: `
  <article class="col-md-12">
    <div>
      <form class="navbar-form form-search"
        (ngSubmit)="search(mediaSearch.value)">
```

```
    <div class="form-group clearfix">
      <input placeholder="Explore Media"
        type="search" class="form-control" autocomplete="off"
        [value]="searchQuery" #mediaSearch name="mediaSearch">
    </div>
  </form>
</div>
<code>
  There are {{ (videos$ | async).length }} videos
</code>
<ul class="list-unstyled">
  <li *ngFor="let video of (videos$ | async)">
    <img [src]="video.snippet.thumbnails.default.url">
    {{ video.snippet.title }}
  </li>
</ul>
</article>

})
```

Now the component's template includes a form with a single input element. The form's "submit" event is bound to the search function in the youtube-videos component class. Now, whenever the user hits Enter to search while in the input box, the search function will invoke the search method of the youtubeSearch service, which is available in this class.

```
ngOnInit() {
    this.videos$ = this.store.select(state => state.videos);
}
search (query: string) {
    this.youtubeSearch.search(query, false).then(response => {

this.store.dispatch(this.youtubeVideosActions.addVideos(response.items));
    });
}
```

Once a response has been returned, I use the dispatch method of the store to invoke the action of "addVideos()". Since we already connected the videos$ property to the store's videos reducer - using the store's "select" method, the reactive nature of observable is triggered, and the new search results will be rendered in this component's template.

Composition of Other Components

Currently, this component's template is quite large, and if we add more HTML code, it becomes hard to maintain and manage. This is a good indication that it's time to rethink the architecture of this component and try to separate concerns.

The search form feature may be a good fit as a component of its own, and we might be able to enhance it with other features (suggestions, filters, etc.).

We might want to create a component for a video file so as to present it with more style. Moreover, since the core of this application is the display of media files, it may be a good fit for a component such as youtube-media.

Finally, it is a good practice to divide large templates into components. Each should have a purpose and should encapsulate boilerplate that can be reused or a boilerplate that would be simpler to maintain when it is part of a dedicated component's template.

A good example that may fit in here would be the following:

```
@Component({
  selector: 'youtube-videos',
  template: `
    <player-search
        [query]="playerSearch$ | async"
        (change)="resetPageToken()"
        (search)="search($event)"
    ></player-search>
    <youtube-list
        [list]="videos$ | async"
        (play)="playSelectedVideo($event)"
        (queue)="queueSelectedVideo($event)"
    ></youtube-list>
`
})
```

Now, this looks quite nicer than the bloated template that we had before. It's clearer exactly what this component is composed of, and it's easier to isolate functionality. Later in this chapter, we will refactor this component's template into these components.

In addition, we take can advantage of Angular's change-detection mechanism and boost the performance of our application by updating smaller parts of our component (we'll see how later in this chapter). For example, if only the videos$ reducer has changed, Angular will update only it and will render the appropriate change, and not update player-search as well, even though both components are under the same parent container component.

Stateful Component

We are using ngrx/store to manage a state. An important key concept to remember when composing components is to keep it as stateless as possible. However, whenever we create container components that are responsible for fetching data, there is a good chance we will be defining placeholders for state. These placeholders, as we've seen in the youtube-videos component, will be connected to the store with the preliminary select function, indicating which piece of information should be returned.

Whenever we manage a state in the form of selecting it from the store or dispatching an update to the store, this means that the component is stateful.

There are exceptions where non-container components may manage an internal state. Usually, this state cannot be connected to the application's state (think of the video component—we don't save the actual video's contents, but rather it source path), so there are times when we define internal placeholders (or properties) that may help with a component's functionality.

The purpose of managing a state in a container component is to have a central point where state can be accessed, where actions such as updating or retrieving the state for the rest of the nested components are done. It's easy to look into data flow and track behavior when needed.

Handle Internal Component's Events and Async Operations

When a container component manages the state, it is responsible for updating the application's state when dispatching actions. Taking the previous template as an example, where the youtube-videos component is composed of two components, the template passes JavaScript callbacks so it can interact with the store when a certain event has happened.

These callbacks may result in asynchronous operations, such as searching the YouTube API (this might take time). In return, we will update the store. However, in order to update the internal state of this component, we use must use the async pipe.

It's important to understand that these callbacks actually mark a path for Angular's change-detection mechanism, which should be updated.

Async Pipe

In reactive applications where data may be updated over time, we want the view to update once data has changed. We already took care of that by selecting the relevant store's reducer. This is the part where we ask to listen to the changes made to a store's portion and ask to update the reference we've created to this reducer, as is done in the videos$ observable property:

```
ngOnInit() {
    this.videos$ = this.store.select(state => state.videos);
}
```

As I explained in the previous chapter, in order to use this automatic update in this component's view, we need to use the async pipe. This is usually done in a container component:

```
@Component({
  selector: 'youtube-videos',
  template: `
    <player-search
       [query]="playerSearch$ | async"
       (change)="resetPageToken()"
       (search)="search($event)"
    ></player-search>
    <youtube-list
       [list]="videos$ | async"
       (play)="playSelectedVideo($event)"
       (queue)="queueSelectedVideo($event)"
    ></youtube-list>

})
```

The template will be updated only after the data has been extracted from the asynchronous operation. In addition, whenever this view is destroyed, Angular's mechanism knows it needs to unsubscribe the view from these async listeners.

■ **Note** If you choose to subscribe within the Typescript class, remember you should unsubscribe manually when finished. The returned object of the subscribe method includes an unsubscribe method. This should be triggered within the NgDestroy lifecycle method in the class.

In this template, there are two components that are eventually handled by the youtube-videos component.

The player-search component, which allows you to change the query that will be searched for with YouTube's API, is connected to youtube-videos component, both with the store and with callbacks:

1. playerSearch$ is a new reducer in the store.

2. A "change" event is triggered when the input element is changed.

3. A "search" event is triggered when the user hits Enter or press the Search button.

The youtube-list component's purpose is to render a list of videos (array of objects). This component encapsulates the display template of YouTube videos. It is connected via these properties:

1. A `videos$` reducer provides the current search results.

2. A "play" event is triggered when the user clicks a thumbnail of the video.

3. A "queue" event is triggered when the user clicks the "Queue" text.

Now, that we understand what a container component is, let's add another container component to Echoes Player.

now-playing Container Component

Files This section refers to the src/app/now-playing directory.

Considering there is an already now-playlist reducer, we'll create a container component that will be placed in the sidebar of the application. Its main purpose is to display the currently played playlist. To break it down, it includes a few features:

1. It displays a list of videos the user chose to play.

2. It should indicate the currently or last-selected video.

3. It should allow the user to remove a video from the list.

4. It should allow the user to filter the now playing playlist.

Given this set of requirements, we can start to construct the component. First, we can define a higher level of abstraction from the current template for this component:

```
@Component({
  selector: 'now-playing',
  template: `
  <div class="sidebar-pane">
    <now-playlist-filter
      [playlist]="nowPlaylist$ | async"
      (clear)="clearPlaylist()"
      (filter)="updateFilter($event)"
      (reset)="resetFilter()"
    ></now-playlist-filter>
    <now-playlist
      [playlist]="nowPlaylist$ | async"
      (select)="selectVideo($event)"
      (remove)="removeVideo($event)"
    ></now-playlist>
  </div>
  `
})
```

Similar to the youtube-videos component, since the now-playing component is a container component, I need to use the async pipe in its template to make sure each update of the now-playlist reducer is passed into the components as well as to make sure the components will render only when data has been extracted.

It's easier to maintain this component's main features using a composition of two nested components:

1. now-playlist-filter

2. now-playlist

Following the container component approach, the class of this component should do the following:

1. Connect to the now-playlist reducer in the application's store.

2. Handle the various events that the inner components emit.

With this component, I chose to follow a different approach, encapsulating the interaction with the store in a service. This approach allows us to maintain a code that is completely agnostic to the store's existence and implementation. This is useful for testing as well as for experimenting in the future with other store implementations.

```
export class NowPlaying implements OnInit {
  public nowPlaylist$: Observable<YoutubeMediaPlaylist>;

  constructor(
    public nowPlaylistService: NowPlaylistService,
  ) {}
  ngOnInit() {
    this.nowPlaylist$ = this.nowPlaylistService.playlist$;
  }
  selectVideo (media: GoogleApiYouTubeVideoResource) {
    this.nowPlaylistService.updateIndexByMedia(media.id);
  }
  updateFilter (searchFilter: string) {
    this.nowPlaylistService.updateFilter(searchFilter);
  }
  resetFilter () {
    this.nowPlaylistService.updateFilter('');
  }
  clearPlaylist () {
    this.nowPlaylistService.clearPlaylist();
  }
  removeVideo (media) {
    this.nowPlaylistService.removeVideo(media);
  }
}
```

Now Playlist Service

Most of the functions available in the nowPlaylistService class interact with the store, so an event is dispatched with the relevant event type and an optional payload.

In this code snippet of the nowPlaylistService class, we can see a few approaches:

1. I defined a selector for the nowPlaylist reducer, exported as a playlist$ property.

2. Functions of this class (a few) dispatch actions to the store with the nowPlaylistActions action creator.

```
@Injectable()
export class NowPlaylistService {
  public playlist$: Observable<YoutubeMediaPlaylist>;

  constructor(
    public store: Store<EchoesState>,
    private nowPlaylistActions: NowPlaylistActions
  ) {
    this.playlist$ = this.store.select(state => state.nowPlaylist);
  }

  queueVideos(medias: GoogleApiYouTubeVideoResource[]) {
    this.store.dispatch(this.nowPlaylistActions.queueVideos(medias));
  }

  removeVideo(media) {
    this.store.dispatch(this.nowPlaylistActions.removeVideo(media));
  }
  selectVideo(media) {
    this.store.dispatch(this.nowPlaylistActions.selectVideo(media));
  }
}
```

Now Playlist Actions

This class plays an important role when working with ngrx/store.

First, it includes all the available actions that the now-playlist reducer should handle. These actions are defined as "static" properties, so can be read simply by accessing the namespace of the class following the action property name:

```
selectVideo(media: GoogleApiYouTubeVideoResource): Action {
    return {
      type: NowPlaylistActions.SELECT,
      payload: media
    };
  }
```

Second, it includes action creators—functions that return an object of an action. This includes a type property and an optional payload property. This strategy promotes the reuse of code structure when dispatching actions while also taking care of making the code maintainable. It's easy to reason through and track an action when it's created only in one place of the code repository.

This is a code snippet of the NowPlaylistActions class:

```
@Injectable()
export class NowPlaylistActions {
  static QUEUE = '[NOW PLAYLIST] QUEUE';
  static QUEUE_LOAD_VIDEO_SUCCESS = '[NOW PLAYLIST] QUEUE_LOAD_VIDEO_SUCCESS';
  static SELECT = '[NOW PLAYLIST] SELECT';
  static REMOVE = '[NOW PLAYLIST] REMOVE';
  static UPDATE_INDEX = '[NOW PLAYLIST] UPDATE_INDEX';
  static QUEUE_FAILED = '[NOW PLAYLIST] QUEUE_FAILED';
  static FILTER_CHANGE = '[NOW PLAYLIST] FILTER_CHANGE';
  static REMOVE_ALL = '[NOW PLAYLIST] REMOVE_ALL';
  static SELECT_NEXT = '[NOW PLAYLIST] SELECT_NEXT';
  static SELECT_PREVIOUS = '[NOW PLAYLIST] SELECT_PREVIOUS';
  static QUEUE_VIDEOS = '[NOW PLAYLIST] QUEUE_VIDEOS';

  queueVideo(media: GoogleApiYouTubeVideoResource): Action {
    return {
      type: NowPlaylistActions.QUEUE,
      payload: media
    };
  }
}
```

Now Playlist Reducer

The reducer function is the only place in the code where the state of the now playlist is actually changing. As a reminder, usually the reducer function takes the current state as the first argument and an action object as the second argument. Usually, it returns a value that has been processed with regards to the action's type and payload (if sent).

A common way to write a reducer is to use a switch/case statement that corresponds to the action's type. Usually, the default case returns the actual state to mark that there is no change or when the type shouldn't be handled here.

```
export function nowPlaylist (
  state: YoutubeMediaPlaylist = initialState,
  action: Action) {
  let isDifferent = (media: GoogleApiYouTubeVideoResource) => media.id !==
action.payload.id;
  switch (action.type) {
    case NowPlaylistActions.SELECT:
      return Object.assign({}, state, { index: action.payload.id });
```

```
case NowPlaylistActions.REMOVE:
  return Object.assign({}, state, { videos: state.videos.
  filter(isDifferent) });

default:
  return state;
}
```

An important rule of thumb to notice here: the return value should always be a newly created value; let it be an object, array, or other. The current state (the first argument in this function) should not be mutated. This is crucial for the change detection of Angular to work properly.

Now that we've defined the actions for the now-playlist reducer, we can start diving into the components that will consume its state. First, we will review what a presentational component is, followed by reviewing the actual presentational components that compose the now-playlist component.

Presentational / Dumb Component

A presentational component is usually concerned with how things look and behave.

1. Usually includes @Input() attributes as data providers

2. Doesn't mutate data, but rather emits events through Output attributes

3. Has no dependency on the rest of the app

Presentational components are should be used when one or more of these indications happen:

1. Sometimes creating a presentational component may assist in "clearing" a component's template of HTML code that may be easy to encapsulate and manage in a smaller component.

2. When a snippet of code is copied and pasted.

■ **Note**   Files This section refers to the src/app/now-playing/now-playlist and src/app/now-playing/now-playlist-filter directories.

@Input() as Data Provider

Looking at the template of the now-playlist container component, it is easy to see that it is composed of two presentational components:

1. now-playlist

2. now-playlist-filter

Each of these components defines @Input() attributes that it expects to get in order to display something on the screen and to function as expected.

The now-playlist component relies on data coming in from the playlist attribute. It is an object that includes a videos array property, an index property that includes the ID of the selected track, and a filter property indicating a string with which to filter the videos list. Its main role is to display the tracks within this playlist. Let's define this component:

```
@Component({
  selector: 'now-playlist',
  template: `
  <section class="now-playlist ux-maker">
    <ul class="nav nav-list ux-maker nicer-ux">
      <li class="now-playlist-track" #playlistTrack
        [class.active]="isActiveMedia(video.id, playlistTrack)"
        *ngFor="let video of playlist.videos | search:playlist.filter;
        let index = index"
      >
        <a class="" title="{{ video.snippet.title }}"
          (click)="selectVideo(video)">
          <span class="label label-primary fa fa-list-ul playlist-track"
            title="Includes specific cued tracks - soon to come..."
          ></span>
          <span class="track-number">{{ index + 1 }}</span>
          <section class="video-thumb">
            <img draggable="false"
            src="{{ video.snippet.thumbnails.default.url }}">
          </section>
          <span class="video-title">{{ video.snippet.title }}</span>
          <span class="label label-danger ux-maker remove-track"
          title="Remove From Playlist"
            (click)="removeVideo(video)"><i class="fa fa-remove"></i></span>
        </a>
      </li>
    </ul>
  </section>
  `,
  changeDetection: ChangeDetectionStrategy.OnPush
})
export class NowPlaylist implements AfterViewChecked {
  @Input() playlist: YoutubeMediaPlaylist;
  constructor() { }
}
```

Notice how the constructor for this class is empty. It doesn't connect to any store, but rather expects the data to come from the @Input() member decorator - a function that decorates the property that is defined next to it - so it should get its value from outside the component.

Emit Events with @Output()

Presentational components don't mutate data that comes in from @Input(). On the contrary, they should emit an event that will usually describe an action that has occurred inside the component, accompanied by optional data that might be relevant in order for this action to be processed.

The NowPlaylist class defines such two events:

1. select – when a track is selected in this playlist to be played

2. remove – when a track's Remove button has been clicked

```
export class NowPlaylist implements AfterViewChecked {
  @Input() playlist: YoutubeMediaPlaylist;
  @Output() select = new EventEmitter();
  @Output() remove = new EventEmitter();

  selectVideo (media) {
    this.select.emit(media);
  }

  removeVideo (media) {
    this.remove.emit(media);
  }
}
```

Although it might be tempting to handle these operations inside the code, I stick to the rules of state management and dispatch the event to the store for it to handle this operation within the reducer function. Remember: data is not mutated inside these types of components.

However, an exception for this this rule is when you manage an internal state that might be related to how things are rendered or how they function inside this component. For example, when a track is played, I do want the playlist to scroll to it. At this point, the playlist object includes the index property, which is the currently selected track's ID.

In order to scroll the container to the relevant place in the DOM, I chose to use JavaScript's scrollIntoView() method, which is invoked from a DOM element. For this purpose, I have to save a reference to the selected DOM element. This is crucial for this feature to function correctly. To achieve this, whenever this component renders the videos, there is a function that checks whether the media rendered is the currently selected media. This is the point where this component saves a reference to the DOM element as well.

```
export class NowPlaylist implements AfterViewChecked {
  @Input() playlist: YoutubeMediaPlaylist;
  @Output() select = new EventEmitter();
  @Output() remove = new EventEmitter();
```

65

```
  private activeTrackElement: HTMLULItElement;

  constructor() { }

  ngAfterViewChecked() {
    this.scrollToActiveTrack();
  }
  scrollToActiveTrack() {
    if (this.activeTrackElement) {
      this.activeTrackElement.scrollIntoView();
    }
  }

  selectVideo (media) {
    this.select.emit(media);
  }

  removeVideo (media: GoogleApiYouTubeSearchResource) {
    this.remove.emit(media);
  }

  isActiveMedia(mediaId: string, trackElement: HTMLULItElement) {
    const isActive = this.playlist.index === mediaId;
    if (isActive) {
      this.activeTrackElement = trackElement;
    }
    return isActive;
  }
}
```

No Dependencies on the Rest of the App

This rule means that presentational component can be easily consumed in container components (when it's a core component that is shared) or throughout the nested components inside a container component (when it's a nested component that belongs to a feature module, such as the youtube-videos module).

Since presentational component is destined to be reused across the application in several cases, having hard-coded specific dependencies is discouraged and may get in the way.

It's important to note that this rule is relevant for dependencies that relate to data providers and services that are required by the application. The component should not be dependent on ngrx/store, since store injection should only be present in the container components.

There are a few exceptions to this rule, such as: a presentational component may be composed of other presentational components, or a presentational component can include a special service that it uses to function correctly within its own "component sandbox".

Before we move on to another example of a presentational component, it's important to understand Angular's change-detection strategy and how it can influence any type of component as well as integrate the reactive nature of ngrx/store.

ngrx/store and Change-Detection Strategy

With ngrx/store incorporated into the application and into the now-playing container component, we can leverage Angular's change-detection strategy to a more performant state.

The default change-detection strategy within Angular is set to check every component with every change (identified as the "CheckAlways" mode in change detector). Although Angular's change detection is quite fast, with different use cases and implementations, it might become slow.

With ngrx/store integrated, we can set the change-detection strategy to be a more focused check—OnPush. This is usually relevant for presentational components and is set within the @Component() metadata decorator in the changeDetection property:

```
@Component({
    selector: 'now-playlist',
    changeDetection: ChangeDetectionStrategy.OnPush
})
```

The OnPush strategy is related to how change detection is performed with regards to @Input() members of a component. It directs the change-detection mechanism to only check once, when the application is loaded. Afterward, change detection triggers rendering only when these @Input()s are changed. This means that if there is an internal state change inside a presentational component and it is not communicated through an @Output() event that might update the state in a reducer, a re-render will not happen.

An important rule to understand is that in order to trigger change through @Input()s, the value or reference *must* change. This rule eliminates the mutation of objects. This explains why we should always return a new state object and not mutate the old one, as it won't trigger change detection.

Table 4-1 summarizes a few methods that can be used to create a new state object for different state types that the initial state might be.

Table 4-1. *Creating New State for Each type*

State Type	Creating A New State
Object	Object.assign({}, otherProps)
Array	[...theArray] or theArray.concat()
Primitive Types	Just return the same value

With the change-detection strategy of OnPush in mind, we will continue with presentational components and review another example of such a component—the now-playlist-filter component. This component filters the now playlist tracks in reaction to the search term that is typed in its input element.

Creating now-playlist-filter Presentational Component

If you feel experimental or quite comfortable with the information you have read thus far, I recommend you go ahead and create this component just by following the titles, without reading its contents. You can go back to the now-playing component code to review its template so you can understand which inputs and outputs we expect it to have.

Dependencies

The only dependencies this component has are framework-level dependencies. As indicated earlier in this chapter, presentational components usually don't have any hard-coded app-related dependencies.

An exception is the YoutubeMediaPlaylist dependency, which is an interface that is currently located in the core/store/now-playlist path. Still, this doesn't break the rule of "No Dependencies," as it is not a data- or app service–related dependency.

```
import { Component, EventEmitter, Input, Output, ChangeDetectionStrategy }
from '@angular/core';
import { YoutubeMediaPlaylist } from '../../core/store/now-playlist';
import './now-playlist-filter.less';
```

Change-Detection Mode—OnPush

Since the now-playing component is a container component and is composed of the now-playlist-filter and now-playlist components, we should use the OnPush change-detection mode.

This code can be found in this book's chapter-04 branch.

```
@Component({
  selector: 'now-playlist-filter',
  template: `
<h3 class="nav-header user-playlists-filter">
  <span class="text btn-transparent">
    Now Playing <span *ngIf="!isPlaylistEmpty()">({{ playlistLength }})
    </span>
  </span>
```

```
<button class="btn btn-link btn-xs btn-clear" title="Clear All Tracks In
Now Playlist"
  [disabled]="isPlaylistEmpty()"
  (click)="clearPlaylist()">
  <span class="fa fa-trash-o"></span>
</button>
<div class="playlist-filter pull-right">
  <i class="fa fa-search" *ngIf="isFilterEmpty()"></i>
    <i class="fa fa-remove text-danger"
        *ngIf="!isFilterEmpty()"
        (click)="resetSearchFilter()"
    ></i>
    <input type="search" name="playlist-search"
        [value]="playlist.filter"
        #searchFilter
        (input)="handleFilterChange(searchFilter.value)">
</div>
</h3>
`
,
changeDetection: ChangeDetectionStrategy.OnPush
})
```

Defining @Input & @Output

The now-playlist-filter component takes a playlist object as a single input. It exposes three events: "clear," "filter," and "reset." All events emit data of string type. Here is the full code for this component class:

```
export class NowPlaylistFilter {
  @Input() playlist: YoutubeMediaPlaylist;
  @Output() clear = new EventEmitter<string>();
  @Output() filter = new EventEmitter<string>();
  @Output() reset = new EventEmitter<string>();

  handleFilterChange (searchFilter: string) {
    this.filter.emit(searchFilter);
  }

  resetSearchFilter () {
    this.reset.emit('');
  }

  isFilterEmpty () {
    return this.playlist.filter === '';
  }
```

69

```
  clearPlaylist () {
    this.clear.emit('');
  }

  isPlaylistEmpty() {
    return this.playlistLength === 0;
  }

  get playlistLength () {
    return this.playlist.videos.length;
  }
}
```

Now that the now-playing, now-playlist, and now-playlist-filter components' code is implemented, we can inspect it and interact with it in real time within the browser using the devtools extension called Augury.

View Components with Augury

If Augury is installed, the components tree view can be seen in the Augury panel within the devtools, as shown in Figure 4-2.

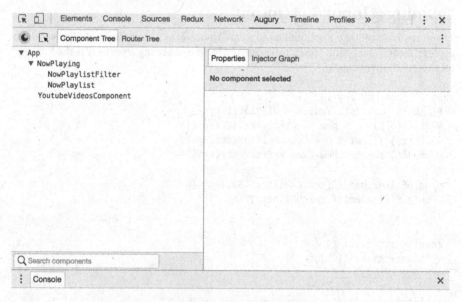

Figure 4-2. Augury displays Echoes' components in a tree view

Inspecting Component

When a component is selected, its inputs and outputs can be viewed on the right-hand side's Properties panels. You can change the value of the inputs simply by pasting or typing it, as shown in Figure 4-3. Moreover, you can emit a component's event with a value simply by clicking the Emit button.

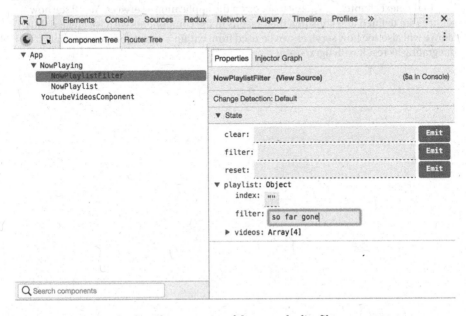

Figure 4-3. Augury displays the properties of the now-playlist-filter component

Summary

This chapter showed you how to create components that align with how ngrx/store works and boost performance for the rest of the application.

Following are key takeaways for this chapter:

1. Use store.select to connect a reducer in container components.

2. Compose a container component out of presentational components.

3. Create stateless presentational components.

4. Use async pipe in the container components' template to automatically pass updated data into presentational components.

5. Use OnPush change-detection mode in presentational components.

6. Always create a new state object. *Don't mutate the state in store.*

7. Follow the practice of dispatching events to the store so data processing and logic are handled in the reducer's file.

In the next chapter, I'm going to focus on the application's services. You'll see how services are defined and consume their results in the components we have created thus far. We will also see how services can be used from within a smart component while integrating its result with ngrx/store.

CHAPTER 5

■ ■ ■

Understanding Services with Reactive Programming

Services are an important building block of any application. Usually, services are the entry point to retrieving data from some kind of provider as well as to updating it, when this option is available.

Services allow the application to interact with remote services in order to perform operations. These operations are usually composed of one or more statements, after which they actually initiate a request out of the application's sandbox.

With ngrx/store included in our application, services play a major role and should be constructed in such a way that it would be easy to connect them to the store while also reusing them in several components within the application.

Services are where you can apply logic, transformations, filters, or combinations. This is a perfect place to apply reactive programming principles with RxJS. We also want to expose services as observable objects so they can fit nicely into the rest of the reactive application.

In this chapter, we will focus on creating reactive services that fit well with the ngrx suite reactive style. We will leverage the power of observables and lay foundations for incorporating a robust layer of data-providing while keeping the architecture of the application neat and scaled in an organized way.

In this chapter, we will create services that allow the application to interact with YouTube's APIs to retrieve data and play videos. The main sections for this chapter will review these concepts.

1. Dive into the search service

2. Review the generic YouTube API's factory service

3. Dive into the YouTube video information service

4. Combine the services we have created in the youtube-videos component

5. Use Angular's "pipes" to transform data before it renders to the browsers

6. Add YouTube Player as a component and a service to play selected videos

7. Write unit tests in the style of Behavior Driven Development (BDD) to a service

© Oren Farhi 2017
O. Farhi, *Reactive Programming with Angular and ngrx*,
DOI 10.1007/978-1-4842-2620-9_5

Diving into the Search Service

Up until now, the Echoes Player (Lite) application has displayed YouTube media items that were returned as a response to a call to YouTube's search API.

When this chapter's branch is served to the browser by running the npm start command in the terminal, the application displays a well-designed youtube-list component that displays a better-designed card for each media item (Figure 5-1).

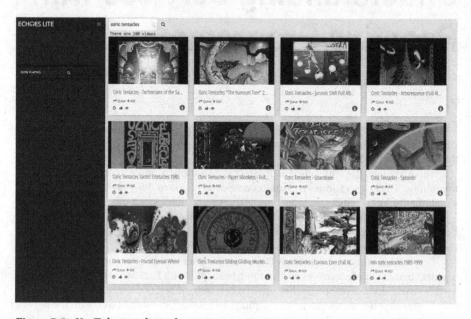

Figure 5-1. *YouTube search results*

Currently, the search service is responsible for querying the YouTube's data API for search results according to the query that is within the search box. This service's implementation is rather short and simple.

In the previous chapter, we used the YouTube search service by injecting it into the YoutubeVideos component. In this example, this service's search method is implemented with the promise API. This API returns a thenable object interface to which we register a function that uses the store in order to dispatch the addVideos method.

```
constructor(
    private youtubeSearch: YoutubeSearch,
    private nowPlaylistService: NowPlaylistService,
    private youtubeVideosActions: YoutubeVideosActions,
    private nowPlaylistActions: NowPlaylistActions,
    private store: Store<EchoesState>
) {
}
```

```
search (query: string) {
    this.youtubeSearch.search(query, false).then(response => {

this.store.dispatch(this.youtubeVideosActions.addVideos(response.items));
    });
}
```

However, contrary to in the previous chapter, in this chapter we're going to update the code of this service so it will use an observable's API rather than a promise API for the search method. Eventually, the following is the code that will be used:

```
search (query: string) {
    this.youtubeSearch.search(query, false)
        .subscribe(mediaItems => {

this.store.dispatch(this.youtubeVideosActions.addVideos(mediaItems));
        });
}
```

YouTube Search Service

The YouTube search service is one of the application's services that connects to YouTube's search API and allows you to search for videos. Let's review this service.

■ **Note** Code can be found in app/core/services file.

Class Dependencies

First, we are going to review the YouTube search service. It is mainly based on another low-level, generic YouTube API service that we can consume and adapt for the YouTube search API. For this purpose, we are using YoutubeApiFactory.create(), which returns a new instance of YoutubeApiService.

```
import { Http } from '@angular/http';
import { Injectable } from '@angular/core';
import { YoutubeApiFactory, YoutubeApiService } from './youtube-api.
service';
```

Class Properties

Next, I define public properties for this service. The url is YouTube's data API for performing search queries. The API property will hold a reference to the new instance of YoutubeApiService. The isSearching property is a Boolean property for indicating whether the API call is in progress. This can be useful for displaying relevant visual progress in the user interface (UI). I also use it later on within this class to initiate another API call, but we'll get to that later.

```
@Injectable()
export class YoutubeSearch {
  url: string = 'https://www.googleapis.com/youtube/v3/search';
  api: YoutubeApiService;
  isSearching: Boolean = false;
```

Class Constructor

Next, let's create the YoutubeApiService instance in the constructor of the YouTube search service. I'm using YoutubeApiFactory.create() to create a new instance.

I'm using Angular's dependency injection, as it allows me to mock up this service for testing as well as replace this factory with another one. After creating the instance, I set relevant options for this API to work properly.

```
constructor(private http: Http, apiFactory: YoutubeApiFactory) {
    this.api = apiFactory.create();
    this.api.setOptions({
      url: this.url,
      http: http,
      config: {
        part: 'snippet,id',
        q: '',
        type: 'video'
      }
    });
  }
```

The setOptions takes a json object with several properties for configuring the new instance.

- http – I chose to design the YoutubeApiService so it can use any HTTP service. In this case, Angular's default HTTP service is used.

- config – this is used to configure the actual request's option arguments that are used when an HTTP is making a request to YouTube's data API.

  - part – indicates which of the resource's properties should be in the response

  - q – placeholder for the actual search query, which we will update according to the search input

  - type – indicates the type of media results to search for

  - url – the url to use for the API

■ **Note** For more information about YouTube's search data API, you can navigate to `https://developers.google.com/youtube/v3/docs/search`. We'll dive into the YoutubeApiService later.

The Search Method

As indicated earlier, this is the main method the application uses to perform a search. This method takes two arguments:

1. query – This is the query string that will be used in the search request.

2. shouldBeReset – We are using this argument in order to reset the request whenever a new query string is passed. This is required since we might want to fetch a few pages (sets of data of up to fifty results), which requires setting config to pageToken. We will dive into this later.

Finally, I'm using the YoutubeApiService.list method, which returns an observable now. I'm using the map operator in this case to update the isSearching property to indicate that the search is done. Using the map operator still returns an observable object.

This is an important concept to recall: the search operation will start only when we subscribe to this function. subscribe starts the execution context, which in this case starts the request.

```
search(query: string, shouldBeReset?: Boolean) {
    const isNewSearch = query && query !== this.api.config.get('q');

    if (shouldBeReset || isNewSearch) {
        this.resetPageToken();
    }
    if (query) {
        this.api.config.set('q', query);
    }

    this.isSearching = true;
    return this.api.list('video')
        .map((response: any) => {
            this.isSearching = false;
            return response.items;
        });
}
```

YouTube API Factory

■ **Note**   This section's code can be found in the app/core/services file.

So far, I have introduced the YouTube search service, which has the purpose of providing searching abilities in the app. If you look at the constructor once again, you'll see that Angular injects two services:

1. HTTP

2. YoutubeApiFactory

I created the YoutubeApiFactory class in order to create a new instance of another reusable service class: YoutubeApiService. Since some of the features of the YouTube API are the same as for other API calls, I extracted the primary common features into a class that turned out to be useful for other API calls, hence reducing code and keeping things DRY.

■ **Note**   **DRY** stands for "Don't Repeat Yourself," which is a good and recommended concept when developing and designing reusable code.

The code for the YoutubeApiFactory service class is rather short:

```
@Injectable()
export class YoutubeApiFactory {
  create(): YoutubeApiService {
    return new YoutubeApiService();
  }
}
```

This allows you to create a few instances from YoutubeApiService, configure them with the right URL of the API, and even set an initial URL search parameter. Using the factory pattern allows you to enjoy several benefits when working with Angular:

1. Using dependency injection (DI)

2. The DI allows you to test and mock up the factory class easily in classes that consume it.

3. Test and mock up the factory class itself

Let's view how we can reuse the YoutubeApiFactory service class in another service. This is also a good chance to see how to combine several services with RxJS.

YouTube Video Info Service

Currently, when searching for videos, the application renders results based on a request made to the YouTube search service. The data that is returned from the YouTube search API doesn't include information such as statistics and duration of the video. The current status of how the application is rendered is depicted in Figure 5-2.

Figure 5-2. *YouTube search results with missing information*

There is a separate API call that we can make to YouTube's video API in order to get the missing information. The next few sections will show you how to create a service whose main purpose is to fetch this kind of information.

Class Dependencies

The dependencies for this class are similar to those of the YouTube Search service. I'm using the same YoutubeApiFactory and YoutubeApiService classes for creating this service.

```
import { Http } from '@angular/http';
import { Injectable } from '@angular/core';
import { YoutubeApiFactory, YoutubeApiService } from './youtube-api.
service';
```

Class Properties

The class is simple at the moment. All we need for this class is an instance of the YoutubeApiService service class.

```
@Injectable()
export class YoutubeVideosInfo {

  private api: YoutubeApiService;
```

Class Constructor

The constructor is similar to the YouTube search service. It creates a new instance of YoutubeApiService with YoutubeApiFactory.

To configure this API for the videos API, I'm using the setOptions() method to define the relevant URL. I also set the part property to request statistics and contentDetails (which includes the duration of the video) in addition to getting the actual snippet–the video metadata.

```
constructor(private http: Http, private apiFactory:
YoutubeApiFactory) {
    this.api = apiFactory.create();
    this.api.setOptions({
        url: 'https://www.googleapis.com/youtube/v3/videos',
        http: this.http,
        idKey: 'id',
        config: {
          part: 'snippet,contentDetails,statistics'
        }
    });
}
```

Fetch Video Data

Next, I add a method that should request, for any given ID, its additional video meta data using the API service that was defined within the constructor. The mediaId argument can be a string of ID—or rather a string of several IDs—separated by a comma (according to the reference in YouTube's API).

```
fetchVideoData (mediaId: string) {
    return this.api
      .list(mediaId)
      .map(response => response.items);
}
```

Integrating Search and Video Data

In this section, we will learn a new transformation function for RxJS. In order to render the list of videos only after the full data is available (statistics and video duration), we need to update the code of the search method in the YoutubeVideos component.

Currently, the component invokes the search method of the YoutubeSearch service class and dispatches an event once the response has been returned:

```
search (query: string) {
    this.youtubeSearch
      .search(query)
      .subscribe(mediaItems => {

this.store.dispatch(this.youtubeVideosActions.addVideos(mediaItems));
      });
  }
```

In order to use the new YoutubeVideosInfo service, we need to follow the steps outlined next.

Add YoutubeVideosInfo in DI

I imported the service and added it as a dependency injection in the constructor:

```
import { YoutubeVideosInfo } from '../core/services/youtube-videos-info.
service';
constructor(
    private youtubeSearch: YoutubeSearch,
    private nowPlaylistService: NowPlaylistService,
    private youtubeVideosActions: YoutubeVideosActions,
    private nowPlaylistActions: NowPlaylistActions,
    private youtubeVideosInfo: YoutubeVideosInfo,
    private store: Store<EchoesState>
  ) {
  }
```

Combine Search and VideosInfo

By now, we know that the fetchVideoData method expects an ID string, or rather a string of several IDs separated by a comma. Since the search method returns an array of video objects, we can use it to extract the ID of each video and create a new array of IDs. This is done with the map operator, which is the same as the map function of an array.

Now comes the interesting part. I'm using the switchMap transformation function. switchMap gets a function that should return a new observable object. Then, it "switches" the stream's return value from this point to carry on the return value of the new observable. Notice that I use JavaScript's array method join(',') in order to create a string of IDs separated by a comma.

Eventually, the subscribe method gets the return value of the fetchVideoData request, which is a new array of videos with statistics and duration metadata.

```
search (query: string) {
    this.youtubeSearch
      .search(query)
      .map((mediaItems: GoogleApiYouTubeSearchResource[]) => mediaItems.
      map(video => video.id.videoId))
      .switchMap((mediaIds: string[]) => this.youtubeVideosInfo.fetchVideoData
      (mediaIds.join(',')))
      .subscribe(mediaItems => {

this.store.dispatch(this.youtubeVideosActions.addVideos(mediaItems));
        });
  }
```

Fine-Tune—Pipes & View

So far, we have created services for our application that allow us to retrieve data from remote APIs. Now, it's time to fine-tune the view in our application and add final touches.
There are a few issues we need to address before we continue:

1. We need to add the duration to each media component.

2. We need to clear the current results if a new search query is used.

3. We need to allow the user to retrieve the next page of results for the same search query (a.k.a. some sort of paging).

Change Service Data with Transformations (Pipe)

We already have the data of the duration property; however, it is returned in the form of ISO 8601. Currently, the duration displays values in this form: PT46M52S. This snippet means that the duration is 46 minutes and 52 seconds. It is not so user friendly.

■ **Note** ISO 8601 is a format that represents dates and times that apply to the Gregorian calendar, based on a 24-hour timekeeping system. For more information, read further at https://en.wikipedia.org/wiki/ISO_8601.

We could change each duration to a friendly readable string; however, mutating a service's data is not such a good idea. We might want to use the original data in different ways across the application.

In order to achieve this, we are going to use a *pipe*. A pipe is a way to transform data before the view renders. It is an expression that is declared within the HTML template and doesn't mutate the actual source data.

■ **Note**   Pipes are known in AngularJS as *filters*.

Creating toFriendlyDuration Pipe

Within the core/pipe directory, I created a new file: toFriendlyDuration.pipe.ts. First, the relevant @Pipe() decorator is imported, which allows us to define the name of the pipe that will be used in the HTML. I also import the PipeTransform interface, which aids at guiding me in which functions I should implement to comply with Angular.

```
import { Pipe, PipeTransform } from '@angular/core';
@Pipe({
  name: 'toFriendlyDuration'
})
```

Next, I define a class with a single transform() method. This method is used by Angular to transform a value to a new value. The transform() method may receive two arguments, as follows:

1. value – This is the actual value of the property that is declared as an expression in the HTML code.

2. args – This argument is an optional parameter that may be used to add more transformation power; i.e., fine-tuning the amount of characters this filter should return.

The actual body of the transform() method is written with a plain JavaScript code. It parses the string it gets from a duration property within the value parameter, parses the string up to the hours (H) time parameter, and returns a friendly formatted time string in the form of 00:46:25 (taking the duration example value).

```
export class ToFriendlyDurationPipe implements PipeTransform {
  transform(value: string, args?: any[]): any {
    const time = value;
    if (!time) {
      return '...';
    }
    return ['PT', 'H', 'M', 'S'].reduce((prev, cur, i, arr) => {
      const now = prev.rest.split(cur);
      if (cur !== 'PT' && cur !== 'H' && !prev.rest.match(cur)) {
        prev.new.push('00');
      }
```

```
      if (now.length === 1) {
        return prev;
      }
      prev.new.push(now[0]);
      return {
        rest: now[1].replace(cur, ''),
        new: prev.new
      };
    }, { rest: time, new: [] })
    .new.filter(_time => _time !== '')
    .map(_time => _time.length === 1 ? `0${_time}` : _time)
    .join(':');
  }
}
```

This pipe is added to the PIPES array, which is defined in the same directory within the index.ts file. The PIPES array is added to the core module within the core/index.ts file. It is added in both the declarations and the exports properties of the @NgModule decorator of the CoreModule class.

Using the toFriendlyDuration Pipe

In order to use this new pipe, we need to declare it within the HTML together with an Angular template expression.

Within the core/components/youtube-media directory, we'll add the new filter inside the youtube-media.html file. Notice that the expression that resolves to the duration property is followed by the pipe character and then the actual pipe name as defined within the pipe decorator metadata.

```
<span class="item-action">
    <i class="fa fa-clock-o"></i>{{ media.contentDetails.duration |
toFriendlyDuration }}</span>
```

After this update in the code, the time duration, the likes count, and the views count should render as in Figure 5-3.

Figure 5-3. All three metadata properties parsed and rendered under each media card

Clear Results When a New Query Is Searched

This step is quite simple to achieve. There might be a few different ways to code this one.

First, let's add a method to the YoutubeSearch service class in the youtube.search. ts file. Actually, the code for this method is taken from the search method, so it's a good candidate for refactoring to clean up the search method and avoid the duplication of code. Now, we can reuse the code, which can tell if a query is new.

```
@Injectable()
export class YoutubeSearch {
    ......
    search(query: string, shouldBeReset?: Boolean) {
        const isNewSearch = this.isNewSearchQuery(query);
        ....
    }
    ......
    isNewSearchQuery (query: string) {
        return query !== this.api.config.get('q');
    }
}
```

Next, we need to update the search method handler of the YouTube-videos component. We will add an if statement within the search method *before* the search method of the YouTube search service is performed, then dispatch an action of RESET to the store of the YouTube videos list.

```
search (query: string) {
    if (this.youtubeSearch.isNewSearchQuery(query)) {
        this.store.dispatch(this.youtubeVideosActions.reset());
    }
    this.youtubeSearch
    .search(query)
    .map((mediaItems: GoogleApiYouTubeSearchResource[]) => mediaItems.
    map(video => video.id.videoId))
    .switchMap((mediaIds: string[]) => this.youtubeVideosInfo.
    fetchVideoData(mediaIds.join(',')))
    .subscribe(mediaItems => {

this.store.dispatch(this.youtubeVideosActions.addVideos(mediaItems));
    });
}
```

From now on, if the user searches for a new query, the previous results will be removed from the YouTube videos list within the store and only the new results will be rendered to the view.

Allow Paging for Results

Paging can be achieved in several ways within the UI. We are going to take a simple approach:

1. Render a Search More button after the last rendered results.

2. Append the results in the UI to the currently rendered results and push the Search More button to the new position.

We are going to use some of the logic that already exists within the YoutubeApiService class, but first let's add the UI changes. I added the Search More button to the YouTube-videos component's template right after the rendering of the YouTube-list component. I added a conditional ngIf directive so as to only display this button when there are results. I'm using async and the same videos$ observable to determine this.

```
<ul class="list-unstyled">
    <youtube-list [list]="videos$ | async"
      (queue)="queueSelectedVideo($event)"
    ></youtube-list>
</ul>
```

```
<section *ngIf="(videos$ | async).length">
    <button class="btn btn-primary"
      (click)="searchMore(mediaSearch.value)">
    Search More
    </button>
</section>
```

This results in the rendering of this button after the results, are shown in Figure 5-4.

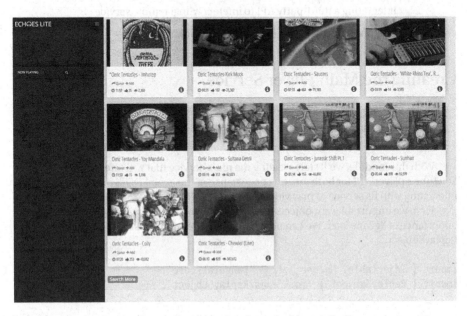

Figure 5-4. *Search More button is rendered at the end of the results list*

Notice I added a click handler to this button. This button invokes the searchMore method inside the YouTube-videos component. This method invokes the searchMore method of the YoutubeSearch service. This method sets the next page token inside the YoutubeApiService class. The code uses setNextPageToken(), which is managed inside this class, so it sets the pageToken property within the search params object.

```
// youtube.search.ts
searchMore() {
    if (!this.isSearching) {
      this.api.setNextPageToken();
    }
  }
```

Notice that this page token should be cleared when a new query is searched. This is a requirement because only then will the API return results with a new page token for the new query. This is currently done within the search method. This concludes the paging support for the search feature; it will handle all cases where the page token needs to be reset.

Adding a Player

It's time to make some noise! So far, we have added the search feature, which allows the user to search and display search results. It's time to add one of the most important features for Echoes—the Player module.

The integration of this player involves several challenges:

1. Integrating a third-party API for creating a DOM element

2. Integrating a third-party API to interact with a remote service

3. Creating a new store for the player component

Creating the Main Player Service

■ **Note** This section's code is in the `app/core/services/player/player.service.ts`.

With this module, we'll start creating the main service that will interact with YouTube's player API for both creating an instance of the actual DOM player and interacting with its service to play videos.

First, we import relevant objects for declaring a service. We will discuss the importance of NgZone later. We can now introduce a new RxJS observable called ReplaySubject:

```
import { Injectable, NgZone } from '@angular/core';
import { ReplaySubject } from 'rxjs/ReplaySubject';
```

The ReplaySubject Observable

The ReplaySubject observable is built on top of the Subject observable. It differs from the Subject observable in that it can record multiple *configured* values from the observable execution and "replay" them to *new* subscribers.

This means that even though a value has been emitted to current subscribers, it can be emitted again to new subscribers of this observable. This feature is important in the context of the player module for a few reasons:

1. We need to load a third-party external script for creating the player; this is an async operation that might take an unknown amount of time.

2. We need to use the YouTube's player API to create a new player; this operation is an async one and may be of unknown duration.

3. A user might choose to play a media item before the player is ready; this is also considered an async operation.

In order to coordinate all of these async operations, the ReplaySubject observable might assist. Let's see how.

First, let's define the Player service class, its constructor, and the ReplaySubject instance. In this case, I need a record side of "1" for the replay, since the YouTube player iframe API is going to be loaded only once for the entire application:

```
@Injectable()
export class YoutubePlayerService {
  player: YT.Player;
  api: ReplaySubject<any>;

  private isFullscreen: boolean = false;
  private defaultSizes = {
    height: 270,
    width: 367
  };

  constructor(private zone: NgZone) {
    this.createApi();
  }

  createApi() {
    this.api = new ReplaySubject(1);
    const onYouTubeIframeAPIReady = () => { this.api.next(window['YT']); };
    window['onYouTubeIframeAPIReady'] = onYouTubeIframeAPIReady;
  }
```

There are a few important code snippets in this code.

The constructor injects the NgZone service. We need this service since we are going to interact with an external service, one outside the Angular application sandbox. Things might change after this interaction. Hence, in order to inform Angular that things have changed and ask it to start detecting changes, we will use the NgZone.run() method.

The createApi() method creates this class main observable. The ReplaySubject observable, "this.api", is used once the YouTube's iframe API has been loaded. The iframe API allows us as developers to create a new instance of the YouTube player.

Now we need the method that will load the YouTube's iframe API script. The loadPlayerApi() method creates a script element and injects it into the document. Once the script is loaded (a "ready" event), the onYoutubeIframeAPIReady function will be invoked by YouTube, which will in return invoke the next() method of the ReplaySubject observable instance. This now emits the window.YT object to every subscriber—those who subscribed before and those who subscribed after this "ready" event.

```
loadPlayerApi() {
    const doc = window.document;
    let playerApiScript = doc.createElement('script');
    playerApiScript.type = 'text/javascript';
    playerApiScript.src = 'http://www.youtube.com/iframe_api';
    doc.body.appendChild(playerApiScript);
}
```

Next, I define methods for interacting with the YouTube player object. These methods use the actual YouTube iframe API that is accessible from the player property. The playVideo() method will load a video by its ID and will play it.

```
play() {
    this.player.playVideo();
}

pause() {
    this.player.pauseVideo();
}

playVideo(media: any) {
    const id = media.id.videoId ? media.id.videoId : media.id;
    this.player.loadVideoById(id);
    this.play();
}
```

Now, we are ready to add the first subscriber. This method receives an HTML ID, which is needed by YouTube's YT object to create the new player instance. Within this method, I created a method that is subscribed to the API. Once the API emits a value, the createPlayer() method runs and, only if the YT object exists, invokes the actual createPlayer() method of the class. The instance of the new YouTube player is saved into the player property.

```
setupPlayer(elementId: string) {
    const createPlayer = () => {
        if (window['YT'].Player) {
            this.player = this.createPlayer(elementId);
        }
    };
    this.api.subscribe(createPlayer);
}

createPlayer(elementId: string) {
    const playerSize = {
        height: this.defaultSizes.height,
        width: this.defaultSizes.width
    };
    return new window['YT'].Player(elementId, Object.assign({}, playerSize, {
        videoId: '',
        events: {
            onReady: (ev) => {
                this.zone.run(() => {});
            },
```

```
    onStateChange: (ev) => {
      this.zone.run(() => {});
    }
  }
}));
```

Great—our service in ready to be consumed and create our player. Now, we will create the player component that will use this service.

The Player Component

> ■ **Note**   This section's code can be found in the app/player/player.component.ts file.

First, we import the relevant core objects that this component is using. Please note that the nest html elements within the template are for style and visibility decisions. The important note to remember is that the "div" which is referred as the "#ytPlayerContainer" is where the YouTube player instance is going to create the actual DOM for the player. YouTube Iframe API creates an iframe instead of it.

```
import { Component, ChangeDetectionStrategy, OnInit, AfterContentInit
} from '@angular/core';

import { YoutubePlayerService } from './player.service';
@Component({
  selector: 'player',
  template: `
  <div class="show-youtube-player">
    <section class="yt-player">
      <div id="yt-player-ng2-component" #ytPlayerContainer></div>
    </section>
  </div>
  `,
  changeDetection: ChangeDetectionStrategy.OnPush
})
```

Next, we declare the class of the player component. This component implements the AfterContentInit() life cycle. Only after the contents of this component are available does this method run. We need this life-cycle interface because the YouTube player instance expects an existing DOM element with the relevant htmlId that is passed to it. Hence, two important setup operations happen in this method:

1. We ask the player service to load the player's API. This loads the YouTube iframe API's external script.

2. Then, we ask to set up the player with the setupPlayer method. This subscribes to the ReplaySubject observable and invokes the internal createPlayer() method to create the instance.

91

```
export class Player implements OnInit, AfterContentInit {
  constructor(
    private playerService: YoutubePlayerService,
  ) { }

  ngAfterContentInit() {
    const htmlId = 'yt-player-ng2-component';
    this.playerService.loadPlayerApi();
    this.playerService.setupPlayer(htmlId);
  }
```

Connecting Player View Components

Now, we are going to update the YouTube-videos and now-playing components so we can select a video and play it on our new player.

Making the YouTube Videos Component Play

First, PlayerService is injected to the constructor. This is a good time to notice that the constructor is getting big; there are too many arguments that it expects. We will deal with this in the next chapter and see how we can reduce it. For the purpose of this chapter, we will still inject this service within the constructor.

```
constructor(
    ....
    private playerService: PlayerService,
    private store: Store<EchoesState>
  ) { }
```

Next, I add the playSelectedVideo(media), which expects a GoogleApiYouTubeVideoResource YouTube media object. Currently, it uses the player service to directly interact with the YouTube player API. In the next chapter, we will use the store and a proper action with a PlayerActions service, but for now, that will suffice.

Usually, as with most media players, when a media is selected to be played, it is added to the now-playlist. We can simply achieve this by calling the method queueSelectedVideo, which is already implemented.

```
playSelectedVideo (media: GoogleApiYouTubeVideoResource) {
    this.playerService.playVideo(media);
}

queueSelectedVideo (media) {
    this.store.dispatch(this.nowPlaylistActions.queueVideo(media));
}
```

Making the Now-Playing Component Play

We are going to do the same for the now-playing component. PlayerService is injected into the constructor and is used in the selectVideo method to play the selected media from the playlist.

In addition, I also want to mark the selected media within the now-playing component if it already exists. For that, I use the nowPlaylistService.updateIndexByMedia() method.

```
export class NowPlaying implements OnInit {
....

  constructor(
    public nowPlaylistService: NowPlaylistService,
    private playerService: PlayerService
  ) {}

  selectVideo (media: GoogleApiYouTubeVideoResource) {
    this.nowPlaylistService.updateIndexByMedia(media.id);
    this.playerService.playVideo(media);
    this.nowPlaylistService.updateIndexByMedia(media.id);
  }
}
```

Now, the application should both play media files and update the now-playing playlist, as shown in Figure 5-5.

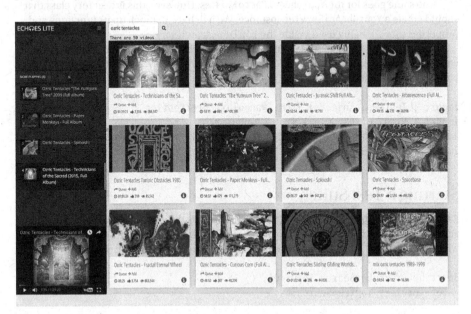

Figure 5-5. *Player is playing a media file, which is marked in the now-playing playlist*

BDD for Services

During this chapter, I mentioned the terms *mocking* and *testing*, together with *dependency injection*. Since services are standard ES6 classes, it's easy to write tests.

Behavior-driven development (BDD) is a software development strategy for writing code with tests. BDD enhances test-driven development (TDD) in that tests are defined from a business perspective and use a more natural language of describing expectations. BDD suggests describing a unit test with simple, plain English.

Writing tests is an important aspect of software development. There's nothing more compelling than seeing those green check marks that tell you that everything is working the way you expect it. However, it's up to you, the developer, to define these expectations and make sure you cover it all.

In this section, I demonstrate how to write tests to our YouTube search service to make sure it behaves the way we expect it to. I'm using Jasmine, a BDD testing framework. Jasmine exposes these global functions to define tests suites, specs, and expectations: describe(), it(), and expect(). You can find out more at https://jasmine.github.io/.

Test Setup

First, import the dependencies that the YouTube search service and the unit tests require. The first two imports from the "@angular/core/testing" package are required in order to set up a testing environment.

Next, since the http service is injected into this class, we need to import the http module; it is used later on in the code.

The same goes for the YoutubeApiFactory class. However, this is a factory class that should create a YoutubeApiService instance. We will have to mock up its functions and properties that are being used inside the YouTube search service.

Eventually, I import YoutubeSearch, the actual service that is tested. The actual class will be used in order to create a new instance, which will be asserted with expectations later in this unit test file.

```
import { TestBed, inject } from '@angular/core/testing';
import { Http, HttpModule } from '@angular/http';
import { YoutubeApiFactory, YoutubeApiService } from './youtube-api.service';
import { YoutubeSearch } from './youtube.search';
```

Starting a Test Suite

Each test suite starts with a describe() statement. This describes the test suite, which is actually a function that includes one or more tests within. I define the service variable, which is accessible for all the following tests that will be written inside this function.

```
describe('Youtube Search Service', () => {
  let service: YoutubeSearch;
```

Next, I use Jasmine's `beforeEach()` life-cycle hook. It's a function that is mostly used for setting up the required state for each test that is going to run inside this `describe()` suite that we have defined.

```
beforeEach(() => {
```

Now, we need to set up objects that we expect to check and run before we create the instance of the YoutubeSearch service. I'm going to use Jasmine's "spy."

A *spy* is a mocked-up object that includes special mocked-up functions that can be tracked by Jasmine. We can use spies to tell whether a function has been called, how many times it has been called, whether it has been called with parameters, and even whether it has been called with specific parameters.

I set up one spy for YoutubeApiService. I don't want to actually test this service at this stage, but rather I need its API interface, since it's being used inside the YouTube search class. I'm using the `createSpyObj()` function to create a spy object with those special functions that I can track.

I created a simple YoutubeApiFactory object as a replacement for the real class.

```
let youtubeApiServiceSpy = jasmine.createSpyObj('youtubeApiServiceSpy',
  [ 'setOptions', 'setConfig', 'isNewSearchQuery',
'setNextPageToken', 'resetPageToken' ]
);
const youtubeApiFactory = {
  create: () => youtubeApiServiceSpy
};
```

The YoutubeSearch class uses the `list()` function in order to perform the actual search to YouTube's API. I don't really want to make this request each time I test, so I mock up this function, which should return an observable API-like object. Since I only need the map function from this API, this can be easily mocked up by creating a simple object with a map function that gets a function as a parameter and invokes it with a return value.

I do the same for the `config` property, which is an instance of Angular's URLSearchParams. This class aids in creating a map-like object for URLsearch is a parameter. It exposes set and get methods for parameters, which are used inside the YoutubeApiService class.

```
youtubeApiServiceSpy.list = (val) => {
  return {
    map: (fn) => fn({ items: [ 'mock' ] })
  };
};
youtubeApiServiceSpy.config = {
  q: '',
  get: (q) => youtubeApiServiceSpy.config.q,
  set: (q) => youtubeApiServiceSpy.config.q = q
};
```

There is another way to spy on objects. Here, I'm attaching a spy to track calls of the isNewSearchQuery and resetPageToken functions of the YoutubeSearch class. I still want these functions to execute the code, so I use Jasmine's .and.callThrough() to make sure these functions will be executed.

```
spyOn(YoutubeSearch.prototype, 'isNewSearchQuery').and.callThrough();
spyOn(YoutubeSearch.prototype, 'resetPageToken').and.callThrough();
```

The code that closes this beforeEach function creates the environment for this test. This is where a module for testing purposes is created using the TestBed class. This is also where I instruct Angular to inject a different object instead of the actual implementation of YoutubeApiFactory. In this case, since YoutubeApiFactory is a class, Angular instantiates it by default using the new operator and then injects the instance. However, I use useValue in order to place the object youtubeApiFactory that I created before so Angular can just inject this object and skip the instantiation process.

```
TestBed.configureTestingModule({
    imports: [ HttpModule ],
    providers: [
      YoutubeSearch,
      { provide: YoutubeApiFactory, useValue: youtubeApiFactory },
    ]
  });
});
```

To conclude the testing environment setup process, we need to retrieve the actual YouTube-search instance. We can do that using the inject function that was imported. This function does the same thing as the decorator @Inject() does; however, as of the time of writing, the decorator cannot be used when writing tests. Inject can be used in Jasmine's beforeEach and it functions. It's as if we inject this service in a component's constructor.

An important note here: for keeping the code DRY and *not* repeating this injection in every test that follows, I chose to save the instance in the service variable that is accessible to all the tests inside this suite.

```
beforeEach(inject([YoutubeSearch], (youtubeSearch) => {
    service = youtubeSearch;
}));
```

I like to start by checking the constructor. In this case, the constructor should create an instance using YoutubeApiFactory. The actual expectation checks that the API property is defined.

```
it('should have an api instance', () => {
    const actual = service.api;
    expect(actual).toBeDefined();
  });
```

Next, I want to make sure that the search method performs two important operations:

1. It should check whether the new query is different (new).

2. It should reset the page token when the query is new.

In this test, I'm using Jasmine's toHaveBeenCalled() matcher (function) with the actual function calls to isNewSearchQuery and resetPageToken. This is where the spy I set earlier comes in handy.

```
it('should should check if query is new before search', () => {
    const actual = service.isNewSearchQuery;
    service.search('ozrics');
    expect(actual).toHaveBeenCalled();
});

it('should reset page token when query is new', () => {
    const query = 'ozrics';
    service.search(query);
    const actual = service.resetPageToken;
    expect(actual).toHaveBeenCalled();
});
```

The last test that I want to show as an example of expressing a "false" expectation is for the searchMore functionality. This time, It should *not* set the next page token of the API property when the searchMore function is invoked while the YouTube search service is in "search" mode.

```
it('should NOT set the next page token when searching and asked to search
more', () => {
    const query = 'ozrics';
    service.searchMore();
    const actual = service.api.setNextPageToken;
    expect(actual).not.toHaveBeenCalled();
});
```

This concludes the testing for the YouTube search service. Tests solve a huge headache while developing. Instead of running these scenarios manually over and over again, the process becomes automated and documented. Also, writing tests ensures we run all scenarios over and over again without skipping anything important. The quality of our application, its tests cycle, and the level of functionality significance are upgraded. Seeing all the green checkmarks is a beautiful picture (Figure 5-6).

```
Youtube Search Service
  ✓ should have an api instance
  ✓ should should check if query is new before search
  ✓ should reset page token when query is new
  ✓ should NOT set the next page token when searching and asked to search more
The Now Playlist Reducer
  ✓ should return current state when no valid actions have been made
  ✓ should select the chosen video
  ✓ should queue the selected video to the list
The Youtube Videos reducer
  ✓ should return current state when no valid actions have been made
  ✓ should ADD videos
  ✓ should empty the state when RESET
  ✓ should replace add new 50 objects when updating data when state is empty
  ✓ should replace 50 objects when updating data when state is not empty

Finished in 0.165 secs / 0.131 secs

SUMMARY:
✓ 12 tests completed
```

Figure 5-6. *Player is playing a media file, and it's marked in the now-playing playlist*

Summary

This concludes the chapter on creating services and incorporating the power of RxJS. I talked about creating services of several perspectives, as follows:

1. Creating a reusable injectable service

2. Using a factory for creating an instance

3. Using a service as a "proxy" to interact with a third-party API

4. Introduction to ReplaySubject, a "recordable" special observable

5. Writing tests for services

   In the next chapter, I'm going to focus on the architecture side of the application—organizing and simplifying the application's code. As our application is getting bigger and bigger, we should keep an eye on how it is structured, which layers the architecture is composed of, and what the role of each layer is. I plan to minimize the responsibility and amount of code in components while introducing a new dedicated layer for mostly async operations as well as a bit of logic, which will be connected to the reactive flow that we have implemented thus far with the store.

CHAPTER 6

■ ■ ■

Managing Side Effects with ngrx/effects

Accompanied Code This chapter's boilerplate code can be found in the chapter-06 branch.

In the previous chapter, our application grew into a functional application. We added more features, which resulted in more async operations. We use ngrx/store to dispatch events. We already saw that some actions might lead to more async actions, regardless of whether it's store actions or service actions.

As it stands, our application might get bigger, and the youtube-videos component is already able to handle more responsibilities beyond receiving state and displaying it.

When one action leads to one or more other actions, it is considered to be a side effect. In order to mitigate this situation and manage the code in a much saner way, ngrx/effects comes into play.

ngrx/effects is another tool under the ngrx extensions suite and dictates a way to manage side effects for ngrx/store actions. It uses RxJS to hook into the store's observable stream and create a new action from an old action.

In this chapter, we will focus on redesigning some of the logic in our application using ngrx/effects. We will create a more robust structure for our application and will define a solid layer for managing side effects.

Introduction to ngrx/effects

The ngrx/effects library was developed as a solution for managing side effects when working with ngrx/store. Similar to ngrx/store, which was inspired by Redux, there were a few libraries that already suggested a way to manage side effect, such as redux-saga (https://github.com/redux-saga/redux-saga).

Let's review how we can use the features of the ngrx/effect extension in order to define side effects in our code.

@Effect() Decorator

@Effect() is a decorator for defining the source of an action while marking a class's method or property as an effect. Once connected to the store's stream, a specific action can be interrupted and transform the stream to a new action.

© Oren Farhi 2017
O. Farhi, *Reactive Programming with Angular and ngrx*,
DOI 10.1007/978-1-4842-2620-9_6

This is a very powerful concept, as it allows us to declare all async source operations within a dedicated layer of effects. This means that any async operations that the application should perform will originate from this layer of effects.

A *side effect*, in terms of our code and ngrx suite, is an action that should be dispatched in response to a previous action. Optionally, the new action might consider the previous action's payload.

A common use case for a side effect is a login process, described in Figure 6-1. The store dispatches a login action. This action results in the initiation of a request for login to a third-party authorization service. Then, upon response and the status of this request, a follow-up action should be dispatched to the store. This follow-up action should be a login success or login failure action.

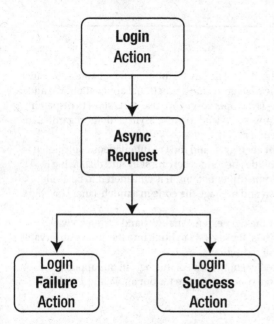

Figure 6-1. Login process with side effects

With code, this snippet may look like this:

```
Class AuthorizationEffects {
  constructor(private actions$: Actions) { }

  @Effect() logActions$ = this.actions$
    .ofType('LOGIN')
    .switchMap(action =>
      this.auth.login(action.payload)
        .map(res => ({ type: 'LOGIN_SUCCESS', payload: res }))
        .catch(err => Observable.of({ type: 'LOGIN_FAILURE', payload: err }))
    );
}
```

This process can be easily coded inside a service or a component. However, this might lead to a complex design in which a component might have a responsibility to initiate the login request (using a service) and handle the response.

@Effect() takes an optional configuration object with a single property, dispatch: boolean-value (true/false), which results in the disabling of the dispatch of an action resulting from this effect. This is useful when there's a need to prevent the side effect from dispatching a follow-up action.

Setting Up and Connecting ngrx/effects

Before we create our first side-effect handler of the application, we'll go through the ngrx/effect setup process. ngrx/effects is a separate npm package that can be installed with this command in the terminal (or command line):

```
npm i @ngrx/effects --save-dev
```

For this project, I'm writing all the effects in the core/effects directory—a class of effects for each feature. There's an index.ts file in this directory that exports an array of these effects classes.

Next, the core module imports this array. In order to connect these effects, each effect (in ngrx/effects version 2) needs to run through the EffectsModule *after* ngrx/store has been bootstrapped. I use the JavaScript array's map method with one linear iteration over the effects array and then run each effect. Notice that the store is initialized within the CoreStoreModule.

```
import { CoreStoreModule } from './store';
import effects from './effects';

@NgModule({
  imports: [
    CommonModule,
    FormsModule,
    CoreStoreModule,
    ...effects.map(effect => EffectsModule.run(effect)),
  ],
  ....
})
```

Creating the First Effect

We'll now create the first side effect for Echoes Player. Usually the effect corresponds to a reducer's actions. I created a youtube-videos.effects.ts file within the core/effects directory.

First, we'll import the relevant packages. The effects class is actually a service that is injectable into our application. I import the Effect decorator from the ngrx/effects package. I also import the Actions class. This class is a stream of all actions that are dispatched to the store from any anywhere in our application.

The toPayload import is a function that simply returns the payload property of the action.

```
function toPayload(action) {
    return action.payload;
}
// or with ES6
const payload = (action) => action.payload;
```

Next, since we're going to add side effects that deal with the current async operations we added to our application, we need to import the relevant YoutubeVideosActions class, the YoutubeSearch service class, and the YoutubeVideosInfo service class. The services are then injected into the constructor.

```
import { Injectable } from '@angular/core';
import { Effect, Actions, toPayload } from '@ngrx/effects';

import { YoutubeVideosActions } from '../store/youtube-videos';
import { YoutubeSearch } from '../services/youtube.search';
import { YoutubeVideosInfo } from '../services/youtube-videos-info.service';

@Injectable()
export class YoutubeVideosEffects {
  constructor(
    private actions$: Actions,
    private youtubeVideosActions: YoutubeVideosActions,
    private youtubeSearch: YoutubeSearch,
    private youtubeVideosInfo: YoutubeVideosInfo
  ) {}
}
```

With this code, we have defined an injectable service that will connect to the ngrx/ store stream using the actions$ - which is an instance of the "Actions" observable - a stream of the store. Before we add effect handlers as properties of this class, let's analyze the code for the youtube-videos component and understand which side effects should be extracted to the effects class.

Extracting Logic from youtube-videos Component to Effect

We have not created the effect yet. We are going to extract the search logic from the youtube-videos component. The reason for this is that the search method has become complex and is responsible for several actions, as follows:

1. It resets the videos array.

2. It initiates a search operation (async operation).

3. It initiates another async operation for fetching additional metadata for videos.

4. It adds the result with an action to the videos array.

There is too much happening in this function. Let's make it clearer and less verbose.

Updates in youtube-videos Component

Currently, we'll focus on the search method alone. It should focus on its purpose—emitting an action of search. Now it is very clear that search has only one responsibility, and it is also quite easy to write a test for it.

```
search (query: string) {

this.store.dispatch(this.youtubeVideosActions.searchNewQuery(query));
}
```

Now, we'll start adding side effects as properties to the new YoutubeVideosEffects class.

Constructing Side Effects to Actions

We will define four side effects on the YoutubeVideosEffects class. As a reference, we'll set each of the preceding numbered logic items to a side effect. A side effect is composed of one or more RxJS operators, as follows:

1. It starts when a certain action is dispatched.

2. It may use operators that filter, transform, or switch to another stream.

3. It must end by returning an action object (i.e., using map).

This is the old code that we will extract to side effects:

```
search (query: string) {
    if (this.youtubeSearch.isNewSearchQuery(query)) {
      this.store.dispatch(this.youtubeVideosActions.reset());
    }
    this.youtubeSearch
      .search(query)
      .map((mediaItems: GoogleApiYouTubeSearchResource[]) => mediaItems.
      map(video => video.id.videoId))
      .switchMap((mediaIds: string[]) => this.youtubeVideosInfo.
      fetchVideoData(mediaIds.join(',')))
      .subscribe(mediaItems => {

this.store.dispatch(this.youtubeVideosActions.addVideos(mediaItems));
      });
  }
```

In the following sections, we will add the effects to the YoutubeVideosEffects class. Keep in mind that these effects, when defined as properties, will run within the constructor phase of this class.

Side Effect: Reset Videos Array

The reset() method should be invoked before the search action is emitted *only* if the query value is a new value in order to empty the videos array so it won't include any previous, unrelated results. Clearly, it's a side effect of the search action.

```
@Effect()
resetVideos$ = this.actions$
    .ofType(YoutubeVideosActions.SEARCH_NEW_QUERY)
    .map(toPayload)
    .filter((query: string) => this.youtubeSearch.isNewSearchQuery(query))
    .map(() => this.youtubeVideosActions.reset());
```

Using the ofType() method, the preceding code will run only after the SEARCH_NEW_QUERY action has been dispatched. Since this.actions$ is an observable, the ofType() method returns this observable sequence, a fact that allows us to continue to use any RxJS operators. I'm using the filter operator to make sure the reset action will be dispatched only if the query value is new.

Side Effect: Search with YouTube Search Service

To perform the actual search, we'll use the same youtubeSearch.search() method that was used in previous chapters. With ngrx/effects, we can create multiple effects to the same action; after all, it's an observable sequence that we can connect to as many times as we'd like.

But before we add the code, we will add two new actions to the youtube-videos.actions.ts file:

1. SEARCH_START – This will be responsible for invoking the youtubeSearch.search() method.

2. SEARCH_ENDED_SUCCESS – This will announce that the search has been ended successfully. This can also become handy if we want to display a "spinner" to indicate that something happens in the background.

```
static SEARCH_ENDED_SUCCESS = '[YoutubeVideos] SEARCH_ENDED_SUCCESS';
static SEARCH_START = '[YoutubeVideos] SEARCH_START';
.....
searchEndedSuccess(items: GoogleApiYouTubeSearchResource[]): Action {
    return {
      type: YoutubeVideosActions.SEARCH_ENDED_SUCCESS,
      payload: items
    };
  }
```

```
searchStart(query: string): Action {
    return {
      type: YoutubeVideosActions.SEARCH_START,
      payload: query
    };
  }
```

First, I decided to create a side effect that might be reusable with the searchMore() feature. This side effect transforms the action of the search to an action that will emit the action creator searchStart().

```
@Effect()
  startSearch$ = this.actions$
    .ofType(YoutubeVideosActions.SEARCH_NEW_QUERY)
    .map(toPayload)
    .map((query) => this.youtubeVideosActions.searchStart(query));
```

In another side effect, we actually need to initiate an async operation—the actual search on YouTube. We need to tell the observable sequence that it is time to switch to a new observable sequence that should emit its value from now on. This is where switchMap fits in. An important note to make at this point is that the switchMap operator stops any previous requests that it started, then starts a new one.

Once the response of the search method has returned successfully, I map the items array to a new array of video IDs. I chose to invoke the new action creator searchEndedSuccess so I can handle its side effect in another isolated sequence.

```
@Effect()
searchVideos$ = this.actions$
    .ofType(YoutubeVideosActions.SEARCH_START)
    .map(toPayload)
    .switchMap((query: string) => this.youtubeSearch.search(query))
    .map((mediaItems) => mediaItems.map(video => video.id.videoId))
    .map((mediaIds) => this.youtubeVideosActions.searchEndedSuccess(mediaIds));
```

Side Effect: Fetching Metadata and Adding the Videos

Great, we are almost there! Now, we need to connect the second async operation, which is responsible for fetching the additional metadata for each video. I'm using here the same switchMap operator to switch the observable sequence to the one of the youtubeVideosInfo.fetchVideoData() method. I took an extra step in here before the switchMap call, converting the mediaIds into a comma-separated string of IDs.

Eventually, after the fetchVideosData() request has returned successfully, we can add the videos response with the addVideos() method. Optionally, we can take another step and dispatch an action to announce the metadata is ready. For now, we'll keep it short and just stick with the addVideos() action.

```
@Effect()
fetchMetadata$ = this.actions$
    .ofType(YoutubeVideosActions.SEARCH_ENDED_SUCCESS)
    .map(toPayload)
    .map((mediaIds) => mediaIds.join(','))
    .switchMap((mediaIds) => this.youtubeVideosInfo.fetchVideoData(mediaIds))
    .map((videos) => this.youtubeVideosActions.addVideos(videos));
```

This sums up the side effects for the search action. We created four side effects that should happen whenever a search action is emitted. Let's see how we can reuse some of these side effects.

Side Effect: The Search More Feature

The Search More feature is currently composed of two statements in the youtube-videos component:

```
searchMore (query: string) {
    this.youtubeSearch.searchMore();
    this.search(query);
}
```

This is a good candidate for a side effect. We should dispatch an action of searchMore and let a side effect initiate the search operation. We already have such a side effect, so we can use it. The searchMore() method should now be:

```
searchMore (query: string) {
    this.store.dispatch(this.youtubeVideosActions.searchMore());
}
```

For this code to function properly, we need to add the search more action and action creator to the youtube-videos.actions.ts file:

```
static SEARCH_MORE = '[YoutubeVideos] SEARCH_MORE';
searchMore(): Action {
    return {
      type: YoutubeVideosActions.SEARCH_MORE
    };
}
```

There is a piece of code that we need to extract from the search method for searchMore to method correctly. The search more process sets the next token string for the API to fetch (by the configuration, it is set to fifty results each time). The next lines within the search() method can be removed. Instead, I added the resetPageToken() call to the resetVideos$ effect with the RxJS mapTo() operator. With it, the second optional argument, shouldBeReset, becomes redundant as well and can be removed.

```
search(query: string, shouldBeReset?: Boolean) {
    const isNewSearch = this.isNewSearchQuery(query);

    if (shouldBeReset || isNewSearch) {
      this.resetPageToken();
    }
....
}
```

The `mapTo()` operator emits a constant value regardless of the source value in the stream. It may become useful if the `resetPageToken()` method returns a value (i.e., a timestamp or the last page token) that can be used to memoize this value for various use cases, most notably to undo the search operation.

```
@Effect()
resetVideos$ = this.actions$
    .ofType(YoutubeVideosActions.SEARCH_NEW_QUERY)
    .map(toPayload)
    .filter((query: string) => this.youtubeSearch.isNewSearchQuery(query))
    .mapTo(() => this.youtubeSearch.resetPageToken())
    .map(() => this.youtubeVideosActions.reset());
```

However, if I chose to stick with the "One Responsibility Rule," I would have created another `@Effect()` while transforming `resetPageToken()` to an observable with `switchMap`, emitting a relevant action, i.e., `PAGE_TOKEN_RESET`.

```
@Effect()
resetVideos$ = this.actions$
    .ofType(YoutubeVideosActions.SEARCH_NEW_QUERY)
    .map(toPayload)
    .filter((query: string) => this.youtubeSearch.isNewSearchQuery(query))
    .switchMap(() => Observable.of(this.youtubeSearch.resetPageToken()))
    .map(() => ({ type: "PAGE_TOKEN_RESET" }));
```

The side effect for `searchMore` will invoke the `youtubeSearch.searchMore()` method. As a side effect of this action, the action of `searchStart()` will be emitted with an empty string. I use an empty string here because the `searchStart(query: string)` method expects a query value. In order to keep the query value within the YoutubeSearch class, the method `search` won't update the q parameter of the API object if the query is of `false` value. An empty string is considered to be a false expression if handed to an `if` statement.

```
@Effect()
searchMoreVideos$ = this.actions$
    .ofType(YoutubeVideosActions.SEARCH_MORE)
    .map(toPayload)
    .map(() => this.youtubeSearch.searchMore())
    .map(() => this.youtubeVideosActions.searchStart(''));
```

Lets see how we can simplify this code implementation.

Retrieving Data from Store inside an Effect

We can make a little bit more effort to reduce the code of the youtubeSearch.search()
method while making the searchMoreVideos$ effect send the actual query value. Using
an empty string seems to be odd enough. We might want to allow the searching of the
YouTube API with an empty string; this returns the latest results. There are two options:

1. Sending the actual query value to the search method

2. Sending a Boolean value

If we are going to support the second option, it will require us to add more logic in
a kind of a hacky way inside the search method or within an effect. Choosing the first
option will reveal a nice addition to the side effects concept. This requires us to rethink
the design of the videos reducer.

Reducer Refactoring

Currently, the videos reducer is an array of YouTube item results. In the long run, it may
be worthwhile to include the query value as part of a state. We already have a use case
where we need to retrieve the current query value. To achieve that, I redesigned the
videos reducer to be of this interface:

```
export interface EchoesVideos {
  results: GoogleApiYoutubeVideo[];
  query: string;
  isSearching: boolean;
};
```

This requires us to first update the videos reducer function body. I created an
initialState object as a default for the new state.

```
let initialState: EchoesVideos = {
  results: [],
  query: ''
  isSearching: false
};
```

The rest of the adjustments for each case use Object.assign to create a new copy of
the state, while now the results property is the reference for the array of videos.

```
export function videos (
  state: EchoesVideos = initialState,
  action: Action
  ): ActionReducer<EchoesVideos> {
```

```
switch (action.type) {
  case YoutubeVideosActions.ADD:
  return Object.assign({}, state, {
      results: [...state.results, ...action.payload]
  });

  case YoutubeVideosActions.REMOVE:
  return state;

  case YoutubeVideosActions.RESET:
  return Object.assign({}, state, { results: [] });

  default:
  return state;
  }
};
```

While we are making changes in this reducer, it's a good time to add handlers for some of the search-related actions. We'll update the new query property of this reducer's state as well as the status of the search process. These are the rest of the switch cases:

```
case YoutubeVideosActions.SEARCH_START:
return Object.assign({}, state, {
  isSearching: true
});

case YoutubeVideosActions.SEARCH_ENDED_SUCCESS:
return Object.assign({}, state, {
  isSearching: false
});

case YoutubeVideosActions.SEARCH_NEW_QUERY:
return Object.assign({}, state, {
  query: action.payload
});
```

This also requires us to update the youtube-videos component. We update the type of the videos$ property and its store selector function within the ngOnInit() life cycle.

First, I exported the special type within the youtube-videos.reducer.ts file:

```
export type GoogleApiYoutubeVideo = GoogleApiYouTubeVideoResource | Object;
```

Next, I added the following type within the youtube-videos component:

```
import { EchoesVideos, videos, YoutubeVideosActions, GoogleApiYoutubeVideo }
from '../core/store/youtube-videos';
```

Then, I updated the videos$ property to be an observable of the new
GoogleApiYoutubeVideo array type and its selector. We can also drop the YoutubeSearch
and YoutubeVideosInfo dependency injections from the constructor as they are not in
use anywhere in this component:

```
export class YoutubeVideosComponent implements OnInit {
  videos$: Observable<GoogleApiYoutubeVideo[]>;
  ...
  constructor(
    private youtubeVideosActions: YoutubeVideosActions,
    private nowPlaylistActions: NowPlaylistActions,
    private playerService: PlayerService,
    private store: Store<EchoesState>
  ) {
  }

  ngOnInit() {
    this.videos$ = this.store.select(state => state.videos.results);
  }
  ...
}
```

Before we move on to the search service, we also need to update the unit tests of the
youtube-videos reducer.

Updating Tests for Reducer

With every code refactoring comes the responsibility of updating its tests. If you are
working in TDD or BDD style, the tests should always run in the background in your
terminal, so you should be able to see a red notification when tests result in errors, as
displayed in Figure 6-2.

```
Youtube Search Service
  ✓ should have an api instance
  ✗ should should check if query is new before search
  ✗ should reset page token when query is new
  ✓ should NOT set the next page token when searching and asked to search more
The Now Playlist Reducer
  ✓ should return current state when no valid actions have been made
  ✓ should select the chosen video
  ✓ should queue the selected video to the list
The Youtube Videos reducer
  ✓ should return current state when no valid actions have been made
  ✗ should ADD videos
  ✗ should empty the state when RESET
  ✗ should replace add new 50 objects when updating data when state is empty
  ✓ should replace 50 objects when updating data when state is not empty

Finished in 0.243 secs / 0.205 secs

SUMMARY:
✓ 11 tests completed
⫶ 3 tests skipped
✗ 5 tests failed

FAILED TESTS:
  Youtube Search Service
    ✗ should should check if query is new before search
      Chrome 55.0.2883 (Mac OS X 10.12.2)
    Expected spy isNewSearchQuery to have been called.
        at Object.<anonymous> (webpack:///src/app/core/services/youtube.search.spec.ts:51:19 <- config/spec-bund
        at ZoneDelegate.invoke (webpack:///~/zone.js/dist/zone.js:232:0 <- config/spec-bundle.js:49464:26)
        at ProxyZoneSpec.onInvoke (webpack:///~/zone.js/dist/proxy.js:79:0 <- config/spec-bundle.js:49128:39)
        at ZoneDelegate.invoke (webpack:///~/zone.js/dist/zone.js:231:0 <- config/spec-bundle.js:49463:32)
        at Zone.run (webpack:///~/zone.js/dist/zone.js:114:0 <- config/spec-bundle.js:49346:43)
        at Object.<anonymous> (webpack:///~/zone.js/dist/jasmine-patch.js:102:0 <- config/spec-bundle.js:48843:3
        at ZoneQueueRunner.jasmine.QueueRunner.ZoneQueueRunner.execute (webpack:///~/zone.js/dist/jasmine-patch.
```

Figure 6-2. When tests are failing, a red notification is displayed

In order to fix the reducer's errors, we'll update the code according to the latest changes, which might result in our removing unnecessary tests or updating its assertions.

The videos state is now an object, so we must update the code that creates an initial mocked-up videos state in every spec. To do that, I created a createStateMock function that returns a mocked-up state object. I'm using the ES6 argument default feature to assign an empty array to the results if a value was not sent. This function takes an optional argument of a "results" array, a fact that would make refactoring easy, as described in this pseudo-code snippet:

```
const createStateMock = (results = []) => {
  return Object.assign({ query: '', isSearching: false}, {
    results
  });
};
const oldState = [...mockedState];
// Will become:
const state = createStateMock([...mockedState]);
```

The next update would be to fix any test that referred to the "results" array to refer to the correct reference of the array. For example, the actual.length object would now be actual.results.length.

```
it('should ADD videos', () => {
    const state = createStateMock([...mockedState]);
    const actual = videos(state, youtubeVideosActions.addVideos(<any>Youtub
    eMediaItemsMock));
    const expected = [...state.results, ...YoutubeMediaItemsMock];
    expect(actual.results.length).toBe(expected.length);
});
```

Now that the youtube-videos unit tests are fixed, we can move on to the unit tests of the search service and update the tests that check the resetPageToken() method.

Updating Tests for YouTube Search Service

The tests for the YouTube search service should be updated as well. We refactored the search method and other parts of this class when we created the side effects, so tests must be updated as well.

First, the code that references the isNewSearchQuery method, which has been removed, can also safely be removed. I removed the spec for "it should should check if query is new before search." from the "youtube-videos.effects.spec.ts" file.

Second, the test for checking the reset page token should be updated as well. Because the resetPageToken method invokes the "resetPageToken" method of the api property, we can easily update the test to this:

```
it('should reset page token', () => {
    const query = 'ozrics';
    service.resetPageToken();
    const actual = service.api.resetPageToken;
    expect(actual).toHaveBeenCalled();
});
```

Now, it's time to update the search-more effect so it can retrieve the latest state from the store inside an effect's stream.

Adding the Store to an Effect's Stream

I would like to introduce a new operator of RxJS—withLatestFrom(...observables). This is a combination operator that allows us to combine the latest emitted value of one or more observables (as arguments) with the current stream.

The result of this combination is returned as an array, while each object in the array represents the value emitted by each observable. In order to refactor the side effect of the searchMore action, we can use the withLatestFrom() combination operator like so:

```
import 'RxJS/add/operator/withLatestFrom';
....
@Effect()
searchMoreVideos$ = this.actions$
    .ofType(YoutubeVideosActions.SEARCH_MORE)
    .map(toPayload)
    .map(() => this.youtubeSearch.searchMore())
    .withLatestFrom(this.store.select(state => state.videos))
        .map((state) => this.youtubeVideosActions.searchStart(state[1].query));
```

With this update, we can have a slimmer youtubeSearch.search() method; we can drop the if statement as well:

```
search(query: string) {
    this.api.config.set('q', query);
    this.isSearching = true;
    return this.api.list('video')
      .map((response: any) => {
        this.isSearching = false;
        return response.items;
      });
}
```

Now, we can move on the next side effects class—the now-playlist effects class. This class should handle any side effects related to actions that happen in the now-playlist reducer.

Transforming Non-Observables to Observables

There is more where we can "clean" our youtube-videos component using side effects. The playSelectedVideo(media) method is responsible for *two* roles:

1. Playing a selected media item from the list of results

2. Adding (queuing) this media item to the now playing playlist

It uses the player service to play the selected media and invokes a queue action using the component queueSelectedVideo. This is a good candidate for creating a side effect. The code for playSelectedVideo is currently:

```
playSelectedVideo (media: GoogleApiYouTubeVideoResource) {
    this.playerService.playVideo(media);
    this.queueSelectedVideo(media);
}
```

113

There is also a bug with this code—it doesn't mark the selected media in the now-playing playlist when first loading the player.

Using the same concept as for the search method refactor, I changed this code to dispatch an already existing action (with an action creator) from NowPlaylistActions. selectVideo(). The reducer for this function updates the currently selected video ID. I'm going to create a now-playlist effect class that will handle the actual play action within the YouTube player and queue the media to the NowPlaylistVideos property.

The code that I added to a new file under the core/effects directory imports the required dependencies needed to handle those side effects—PlayerService and NowPlaylistActions:

```
import { Injectable } from '@angular/core';
import { Actions, Effect, toPayload } from '@ngrx/effects';
import { NowPlaylistActions } from '../store/now-playlist';
import { PlayerService } from '../services/player.service';

@Injectable()
export class NowPlaylistEffects {
  constructor(
    private actions$: Actions,
    private nowPlaylistActions: NowPlaylistActions,
    private playerService: PlayerService,
  ) {}
}
```

The first side effect of now-playlist select action queues the selected media to the list so the application will render the updated list:

```
@Effect()
queueVideo$ = this.actions$
    .ofType(NowPlaylistActions.SELECT)
    .map(toPayload)
    .map((media) => this.nowPlaylistActions.queueVideo(media));
```

The second side effect of the now-playlist select action, will use the player service to play the selected media. With this effect, I'm using dispatch: false to indicate that this side effect should not expect to dispatch a follow-up action.

```
@Effect({ dispatch: false })
playVideo$ = this.actions$
    .ofType(NowPlaylistActions.SELECT)
    .map(toPayload)
    .mapTo((media) => this.playerService.playVideo(media));
```

These two side effects fix the behavior for playing, queuing, and marking the current media in the now-playing playlist. It affects the youtube-videos component in two ways:

1. The playSelectedVideo method dispatches only one action; the side effect of adding this video is handled in the now-playlist.effects class.

2. The constructor no longer requires the player service.

```
    export class YoutubeVideosComponent implements OnInit {
  constructor(
        private youtubeVideosActions: YoutubeVideosActions,
        private nowPlaylistActions: NowPlaylistActions,
        private store: Store<EchoesState>
    ) {}
....
playSelectedVideo (media: GoogleApiYouTubeVideoResource) {
        this.store.dispatch(this.nowPlaylistActions.selectVideo(media));
    }
}
```

Since effects classes are services, we can also write unit tests and set expectations for each effect given the action that is dispatched and the payload that is sent.

Testing Effects

Effects can be tested in a way similar to services. In fact, it is important to write tests as we develop, as it can affect the design of the code and clarify its purpose.

Required Imports

First, we need to import the required packages. Similar to the tests setup I did with services, I import inject and TestBed from the angular/core/testing package. I also import the relevant packages injected into the effects class; apart from YoutubeVideosActions, these will be mocked-up for each test case, as we really don't want to search YouTube for each test. Rather, we assume the response is correct (or false) and check the effect that should handle it.

```
import { inject, TestBed } from '@angular/core/testing';
import { Store } from '@ngrx/store';
import { EffectsTestingModule, EffectsRunner } from '@ngrx/effects/testing';
import { YoutubeSearch } from '../services/youtube.search';
import { YoutubeVideosInfo } from '../services/youtube-videos-info.service';
import { YoutubeVideosEffects } from './youtube-videos.effects';
import { YoutubeVideosActions } from '../store/youtube-videos';
```

Test Environment Setup for Effects

As with each test, the describe() function creates a new test suite. I defined two variables that will be used throughout the rest of this suite. These will be assigned with new objects for each test case.

```
describe('Youtube Videos Effect', () => {
  let runner: EffectsRunner;
  let youtubeVideosEffects: YoutubeVideosEffects;
```

In the first beforeEach block, I create a spy for each service using jasmine.
createSpyObj(). With this method, the first argument declares a new key in Jasmine's internal "hash-map"-like spy repository. The second argument takes an array of strings to create stub functions that can be tracked and "spied" on. Finally, I create a test environment using the TestBed.configureTestingModule method for the effects class using EffectsTestingModule as a container module. Each service is provided to this module using the spies that I created by referencing each spy with the useValue key.

Notice that I manually set the isNewSearchQuery method on youtubeSearchSpy so I can tweak its value in order to test both Boolean values (true and false). To do that, I simply set the isNewSearchQuery variable to the required value for the test case.

```
beforeEach(() => {
    const storeSpy = jasmine.createSpyObj('storeSpy', [
      'dispatch', 'subscribe', 'select'
    ]);
    const youtubeSearchSpy = jasmine.createSpyObj('youtubeSearchSpy', [
      'resetPageToken', 'search', 'searchMore'
    ]);
    youtubeSearchSpy.isNewSearchQuery = () => isNewSearchQuery;
    const youtubeVideosInfoSpy = jasmine.createSpyObj('youtubeVideosInfoSpy', [
      'fetchVideoData'
    ]);
    TestBed.configureTestingModule({
      imports: [
        EffectsTestingModule
      ],
      providers: [
        YoutubeVideosEffects,
        { provide: Store, useValue: storeSpy },
        { provide: YoutubeSearch, useValue: youtubeSearchSpy },
        { provide: YoutubeVideosInfo, useValue: youtubeVideosInfoSpy },
        YoutubeVideosActions
      ]
    });
});
});
```

The second beforeEach() block injects the objects that were initialized during the testing module bootstrap process. I save the runner and youtubeVideosEffects objects so I can reference them on each test case.

```
beforeEach(inject([
    EffectsRunner, YoutubeVideosEffects
    ],
    (_runner, _youtubeVideosEffects) => {
      runner = _runner;
      youtubeVideosEffects = _youtubeVideosEffects;
    }
));
```

Now that we have set up the testing environment for the YouTube videos effects class, we can start writing the test cases.

Creating Test Cases for Effects

Each test case should reflect the side effect that should be taken with regards to the source action. If we write the expectations before we start to code, we may find which side effects should be created.

When we refactored the code of the youtube-videos component to use side effects, we already defined the expectations.

Simple Test for an Effect

We'll start with resetting the videos array. Simply put, when we search for videos with a new term, the videos array should be reset.

First, I create the source action whose side effect I'm going to test: SEARCH_NEW_QUERY. Next, I define the action that I expect to be dispatched: RESET. I use the runner object that was assigned in the second beforeEach block. This is an observable that is based on the ReplaySubject, which was introduced in the previous chapter. I use the queue method that emits the source action. To assert the expectation for this side effect, I subscribe directly to the property reference: searchVideos$.

```
it('should reset when searching new videos', () => {
    const action = {
      type: YoutubeVideosActions.SEARCH_NEW_QUERY,
      payload: 'testing'
    };
    const expected = {
      type: YoutubeVideosActions.RESET
    };
    runner.queue(action);

    youtubeVideosEffects.searchVideos$.subscribe(result => {
      expect(result).toEqual(expected);
    });
});
```

Testing an Effect with a Spy

The second test for SEARCH_NEW_QUERY will check that the resetPageToken method has been called. For that, I need to get a reference to the youtubeSearchSpy service class that was injected. I can now use the inject function to get the reference to the YouTube search service. This will return the reference of youtubeSearchSpy, since I instructed Angular to provide the spy object when YoutubeSearch is injected.

Next, similar to the previous test, I create a source action for SEARCH_NEW_QUERY, which is queued to runner. The expectation for this test is to make sure that the resetPageToken method has been called with the actual action.

```
it('should reset page token when searching new videos', inject(
    [YoutubeSearch],
    (youtubeSearchSpy) => {
      const action = {
        type: YoutubeVideosActions.SEARCH_NEW_QUERY,
        payload: 'testing'
      };
      runner.queue(action);
      youtubeVideosEffects.resetVideos$.subscribe(result => {
        expect(youtubeSearchSpy.resetPageToken).toHaveBeenCalled();
      });
  }));
```

Testing Effect with Action Creator

A third side effect for the SEARCH_NEW_QUERY action exists in a separate new side effect: the SEARCH_START action. The expected side effect with this action is the dispatching of a SEARCH_START action with the given query that was sent with the payload.

In this test case, I'm using inject() again in order to inject the YoutubeVideosActions instance. This is a good chance to reduce the code for both the action and expected objects by using the action creators of this class. In this test case, I check that the action that was dispatched from this side effect has been dispatched with the same query value that was dispatched with the action object.

```
it('should dispatch a search start action when searching new query', inject(
    [ YoutubeVideosActions ],
    (youtubeVideosActions: YoutubeVideosActions) => {
    const action = youtubeVideosActions.searchNewQuery('guitar tracks');
    const expected = youtubeVideosActions.searchStart(action.payload);
    runner.queue(action);
    youtubeVideosEffects.startSearch$.subscribe(result => {
      expect(result).toEqual(expected);
    });
  }));
```

Testing Effects with Store and Observables

An important type of testing checks that an effect is the side effect of the SearchMore action, which takes the latest value from the videos object in the store using the withLatestFrom() operator.

In order to test that, we need to mock up the store.select() return value. In order to do that, I updated the code within the first beforeEach() block. I created a mocked-up select() method that uses Observable.of to create a static observable of the state object that is assigned to it—the videosStateMock variable. I added this variable for mocking up the videos state within the store so I can access it and update its properties for the tests.

```
describe('My Effect', () => {
  ....
  let videosStateMock = {
    query: ''
  };
  beforeEach(() => {
    const storeSpy = jasmine.createSpyObj('storeSpy', [
      'dispatch', 'subscribe'
    ]);
    storeSpy.select = () => Observable.of(videosStateMock);
    ...
  });
});
```

In this test, I created an action of SEARCH_MORE to be dispatched. Notice it doesn't carry any payload as the query value, so it should take the query value from the store. In order to test this, I later define the query value by assigning it to videosStateMock. Next, I set the expected action object to be of action type SEARCH_START, carrying the same query value in its payload—in this case, ambient music.

```
it('should start search with the existing query when searching more', () => {
  const action = {
    type: YoutubeVideosActions.SEARCH_MORE
  };
  videosStateMock.query = 'ambient music';
  const expected = {
    type: YoutubeVideosActions.SEARCH_START,
    payload: videosStateMock.query
  };
  runner.queue(action);
  youtubeVideosEffects.searchMoreVideos$.subscribe(result => {
    expect(result).toEqual(expected);
  });
}));
```

This technique is relevant to any kind of operator that should return an observable, such as switchMap, mergeMap, etc. Now all tests are passing, as depicted in Figure 6-3.

```
App
  ✓ should be defined (skipped)
  ✓ should have 3 public services (skipped)
  ✓ should select a video in playlist (skipped)
Youtube Videos Effect
  ✓ should reset when searching new videos
  ✓ should reset page token when searching new videos
  ✓ should dispatch a search start action when searching new query
  ✓ should start search with the existing query when searching more
Youtube Search Service
  ✓ should have an api instance
  ✓ should reset page token
  ✓ should NOT set the next page token when searching and asked to search more
The Now Playlist Reducer
  ✓ should return current state when no valid actions have been made
  ✓ should select the chosen video
  ✓ should queue the selected video to the list
The Youtube Videos reducer
  ✓ should return current state when no valid actions have been made
  ✓ should ADD videos
  ✓ should empty the state when RESET
  ✓ should replace 50 objects when updating data when state is not empty

Finished in 0.224 secs / 0.186 secs

SUMMARY:
✓ 14 tests completed
i 3 tests skipped
```

Figure 6-3. Player is playing a media item, and it's marked in the now-playing playlist

This concludes the integration of ngrx/effects. In addition, the ngrx/effects extension offers more functionality that can be used with side effects.

More API Features of ngrx/effects

The ngrx/effects module includes additional features that might be useful in various cases.

Merging Effects with mergeEffects

You can choose to create an action after any side effect has run. This might be useful if you want to keep a side effects class dedicated to one action class. To make a long story short, you can trigger a side effect or an action of another class by subscribing to an effects class.

In this example, I subscribe to the youtubeVideosEffects class. For any side effects that run, the subscribed function runs and passes the action object that the side effect has produced. I chose to trigger the action creator updateList of the nowPlayingActions for every side effect of the youtubeVideosEffects class, passing the action's payload. Remember: it's important to unsubscribe with an EffectsSubscription instance in the ngOnDestroy lifecycle method.

Note The updateList is just an example of such an action. We didn't create this action in this application's code.

```
import { mergeEffects } from '@ngrx/effects';
...
class YoutubeVideosComponent {
  constructor(
    private youtubeVideosActions: YoutubeVideosActions,
    private nowPlaylistActions: NowPlaylistActions,
    private store: Store<EchoesState>,
    private youtubeVideosEffects: YoutubeVideosEffects,
    private subscription: EffectsSubscription
  ) {}

  ngOnInit() {
    this.videos$ = this.store.select(state => state.videos.results);
    mergeEffects(this.youtubeVideosEffects)
      .subscribe((action) => {
this.store.dispatch(this.nowPlaylistActions.updateList(action.payload))
    });
  }
  ngOnDestroy {
    this.subscription.unsubscribe();
  }
}
```

There is an API for adding more effects to a current subscription using the this.subscription.addEffects([effectsClassInstance]). This is useful if an effects class belongs to a certain module or if it has been injected via a separated injector (other than the app's injector).

A good example of using this feature is when you have an application's common side effects class that might also be handled in a feature module's side effects. Taking Echoes Player as an example, we might have an application-wide action PLAY_MEDIA side effect, which then would be used to play a media item in the application's player. If a side effects class is implemented for YoutubeVideos component, this action would trigger a side effect that would have to mark the currently selected media item in one of the video cards that are displayed with a "now playing" badge.

Summary

In this chapter, I talked about creating a side effects layer for making async requests and separating concerns. We refactored the application's code with these operations:

1. Creating side effects from complex code

2. Testing side effects of several types created with ngrx/effects

3. Refactoring reducers

4. Refactoring unit tests

Following are some important takeaways from this chapter:

- Keep a component's methods as small as possible.

- Dispatch only one action from a component's methods.

- Approach a code challenge with design and tests.

- An effects class is useful for handling async operations.

- Remember to return an observable in a service async method; this is reusable in many cases, especially with an effects class.

- Remember to update tests when refactoring code. If you use BDD as an approach, this will come out on its own.

- It's important to apply the "One Responsibility Principle" for each component, service, and function.

The next chapter focuses on common solutions that involve adding features while applying several good practices for working in Angular with ngrx. I also talk about reactive programming with forms and how it fits nicely with ngrx.

CHAPTER 7

■ ■ ■

Reactive Forms and Common Solutions

In the previous chapter, I introduced ngrx/effects for managing the side effects of actions in a separate layer in our application. ngrx/effects complements software architecture in Angular-based applications and uses reactive programming with RxJS.

It's time to fine-tune our applications and get familiar with more reactive perspectives.

In this chapter, we will focus on using reactive forms for our search feature, applying some useful solutions to common challenges found in Angular applications while using reactive programming. I will introduce more concepts and features of both RxJS and ngrx that may make our code more readable, maintainable, and testable.

Looking Closely at Reactive Forms

Reactive forms are part of a new technique for building and defining forms in a reactive programming style. They do so by favoring the explicit separation of the data model from the UI (template) and constructing it within a component's class code (usually).

Reactive forms are created using the FormBuilder. FormBuilder aids in creating a tree of form-control objects while using directives to bind it to a form HTML template.

Reactive forms events are based on observables, a fact that allows us to observe a form's state for changes and react to those changes.

Choosing to use reactive forms allows us to easily test and validate how forms behave and are displayed in our components. It also allows us to scale and expand the form's model with little effort.

Switching to Reactive Forms

To start working with reactive forms, the current forms module needs to be replaced with the reactive forms module. This can be done in the src/app/core/index.ts file by loading ReactiveFormsModule instead of FormsModule and adding it to the imports and exports arrays within the @NgModule() decorator metadata.

© Oren Farhi 2017
O. Farhi, *Reactive Programming with Angular and ngrx*,
DOI 10.1007/978-1-4842-2620-9_7

```
...
import { ReactiveFormsModule } from '@angular/forms';
...
@NgModule({
  imports: [
    ReactiveFormsModule
  ],
  exports: [
    ReactiveFormsModule
  ]
})
export class CoreModule { }
```

Now that our application loads ReactiveFormsModule, we can start declaring reactive forms within the components code.

Creating a Reactive Search Form

Currently, the Echoes Player (Lite) application has a form for searching videos. This form is template driven and uses an element reference to pass the input value to the search method. In order to switch to a reactive form, I took the following steps.

Using FormBuilder to Create a Reactive Form

FormBuilder is a convenient injectable class for declaring forms. It has shorthand methods for creating a FormGroup and a FormControl, both of which are classes.

First, I injected the FormBuilder class to the youtube-videos component's constructor. I created a property of searchForm, which will hold the reference to the form's model that will be created using FormBuilder.

```
export class YoutubeVideosComponent implements OnInit {
  videos$: Observable<GoogleApiYoutubeVideo[]>;
  searchForm: FormGroup;

  constructor(
    private youtubeVideosActions: YoutubeVideosActions,
    private nowPlaylistActions: NowPlaylistActions,
    private store: Store<EchoesState>,
    private formBuilder: FormBuilder
  ) {
  }
...
}
```

■ **Note**   FormGroup can hold additional nested form groups using the same this.
formBuilder.group() method.

Next, I added a setupForm method to encapsulate the creation process of the form.
Notice that I'm using the group method in order to create a top-level FormGroup. Inside it,
I defined the mediaSearch value that will be bound to the mediaSearch input later. Notice
that in this case the FormBuilder abstracts the creation of a FormControl for mediaSearch
input element. Finally, I call this method on the ngOnInit component's life-cycle hook:

```
ngOnInit() {
    this.videos$ = this.store.select(state => state.videos.results);
    this.setupForm();
}

setupForm() {
    this.searchForm = this.formBuilder.group({
      mediaSearch: ''
    });
}
```

The last step to take is updating the search() method. Now it should take the value
of the user's input from the searchForm reactive form property. To do that, I reference the
this.searchForm.value, which returns the last updated value of the form's data model.
This reflects the values of any form elements that were defined with FormBuilder and
were bound in the component's template. Then, I can simply reference the mediaSearch
value, which holds the input's value.

```
search (query: string) {
    this.store.dispatch(this.youtubeVideosActions
        .searchNewQuery(this.searchForm.value.mediaSearch));
}
```

Now, we can bind the form to the component's template. The update for the
component's template reflects, in this case, two changes:

1. [formGroup] directive – This binds the searchForm model
   declaration with the form. This directive is required in order
   to bind the whole form and its child descendants to the form's
   nested controls.

2. formControlName attribute directive – This is assigned with
   the appropriate property name, which we have defined in
   the setupForm() method, so any value that is assigned in the
   method when the component is initialized will be available
   here (currently, it's an empty string).

```
@Component({
  selector: 'youtube-videos',
  template: `
  <article class="col-md-12">
    <div>
      <form class="navbar-form form-search" id="media-explorer"
        [formGroup]="searchForm"
        (ngSubmit)="search()">
        <div class="form-group clearfix">
          <input placeholder="Explore Media" id="media-search"
            type="search" class="form-control" autocomplete="off"
            formControlName="mediaSearch"
          >
    ...
</article>`
})
```

With this update, you can run the project and experience the same results as we had before, but with less code and with reactive forms implemented.

Enhancing the Form with New Features

I mentioned that with reactive forms we can scale the form's model with little effort. This means that we can add more model data to the form's structure while gracefully adding more features to the application. Using the reactive nature of reactive forms, we can observe when the form's values are changing and react to these changes using RxJS operators.

Adding Presets Form Control

I want to add a presets feature to the application's search so it is displayed as a group of buttons. Each button represents a preset that affects the search query. For example, I found myself searching for "smashing pumpkins *live*." The "live" is a preset that is relevant for other queries as well, so instead of your typing it, there will be a button for that. The view that I'm going to add is described in Figure 7-1.

Figure 7-1. Presets buttons in the search bar

First, I'm going to update the form's data model with the relevant data property—preset. Since these are going to be radio buttons, the value for each button is a string. As a default value, I would like to use an empty string for the "Any" preset, as this is backward compatible with the old search form.

```
setupForm() {
    this.searchForm = this.formBuilder.group({
        mediaSearch: '',
        preset: ''
    });
}
```

We need to add the relevant HTML code to the component's template. Since the interaction with the presets buttons is part of the search form, I appended the btn-group HTML code inside the form element, which is bound to the model's searchFrom property.

```
@Component({
    selector: 'youtube-videos',
    template: `
    ....
    <form [formGroup]="searchForm"
    ....
        <div class="btn-group btn-group-sm">
            <label type="button" class="btn btn-default navbar-btn">
                <input type="radio" formControlName="presets" value="">Any
            </label>
            <label type="button" class="btn btn-default navbar-btn">
                <input type="radio" formControlName="presets" value="full
                album">Albums
            </label>
            <label type="button" class="btn btn-default navbar-btn">
                <input type="radio" formControlName="presets" value="live">Live
            </label>
        </div>
    </form>
```

React to Form Changes

Now comes the part where we can use RxJS. With every change in the presets settings, I would like to update the relevant data and create a new search with the newly selected preset. For this feature to happen, we need to update the application's code with few changes.

1. Update the reducer of the YoutubeVideos component with a new presets property.

2. Create a new action to update the presets.

3. Update the YoutubeVideos component with the relevant handler for presets.

4. Update the search() method in the YoutubeVideos component's side effects class to add the preset.

5. Trigger search when the preset is changed.

Updating the Reducer and Actions

To update the reducer, I added a preset entry to the interface of this reducer as well as updated the initial state object with a default empty string for the new preset entry.

```
// app/core/store/youtube-videos/youtube-videos.reducer.ts
export interface EchoesVideos {
  results: GoogleApiYoutubeVideo[];
  query: string;
  preset: string;
  isSearching: boolean;
}
let initialState: EchoesVideos = {
  results: [],
  query: '',
  preset: '',
  isSearching: false
};
```

The following updates add a case handler inside the videos reducer function, which handles the new action SEARCH_PRESET. This code simply updates the preset in the state object. I also added the updates for adding the new action to the youtube-videos actions class.

```
// app/core/store/youtube-videos/youtube-videos.reducer.ts
...
case YoutubeVideosActions.SEARCH_PRESET:
    return Object.assign({}, state, {
      preset: action.payload
    });
...

// app/core/store/youtube-videos/youtube-videos.actions.ts
export class YoutubeVideosActions {
  static SEARCH_PRESET = '[YoutubeVideos] SEARCH_PRESET';
```

```
            updatePreset(preset: string): Action {
    return {
      type: YoutubeVideosActions.SEARCH_PRESET,
      payload: preset
    };
  }
}
```

Handling Presets Change

The reactive forms approach exposes the form's model as an observable data stream, which we can use as a source to observe and act upon changes. Each FromGroup object has a valueChanges observable property. This is an RxJS Subject that can be operated on with RxJS operators. It's important to note that valueChanges observable emits the whole updated model for every form control.

In order to act upon preset changes, I'm using several RxJS operators and introducing a new operator, pairwise(). This operator allows us to take the previous and the current values that were emitted and emit them together as an array. This is useful to us, as we need to distinguish whether the preset has changed and then dispatch the relevant action. Together with the filter() operator, we can make sure that onPresetChange() will be called only when the previous and current values of the preset form control are different.

patchValue is a method that allows us to update the form controls' values while emitting a notification about it (as if the user has actually changed it). Since the pairwise operator "waits" until there's a second value, I use patchValue to emulate the first value for the preset. If I don't invoke this, when the user selects one of the other presets, the pairwise operator will prevent the stream from going on until it has two values.

```
setupForm(){
  ...
  this.searchForm.valueChanges
      .map((changes) => changes.preset)
      .pairwise()
      .filter((presets) => presets[0] !== presets[1])
      .map((presets) => presets[1])
      .subscribe((preset ) => this.onPresetChange(preset));
  this.searchForm.patchValue({ preset: '' });
}

onPresetChange (preset) {
    this.store.dispatch(this.youtubeVideosActions.updatePreset(preset));
}
```

Updating Side Effects

Currently, the search operation is invoked only with the query's value. In order to add the preset, I need to make an update in the youtube-videos.effects.ts file. I added the latest value of the videos state using the `withLatestFrom()` operator. Then, I updated the `switchMap()` argument to receive an array of states. The state in index zero is the query that was sent with the SEARCH_START action while the state in index one is the whole videos state. I use both states to compose the appropriate query string, which includes the query value along with the preset value.

```
@Effect()
  searchVideos$ = this.actions$
    .ofType(YoutubeVideosActions.SEARCH_START)
    .map(toPayload)
    .withLatestFrom(this.store.select(state => state.videos))
    .switchMap((states: any[]) => this.youtubeSearch.search(`${states[1].
      query} ${states[1].preset}`))
    .map((mediaItems) => mediaItems.map(video => video.id.videoId))
    .map((mediaIds) => this.youtubeVideosActions.searchEndedSuccess(mediaIds));
```

The result for this side effects does exactly what I aimed for—searched in YouTube's data API for the query `chillout` with the "Albums" preset selected, as shown in Figure 7-2.

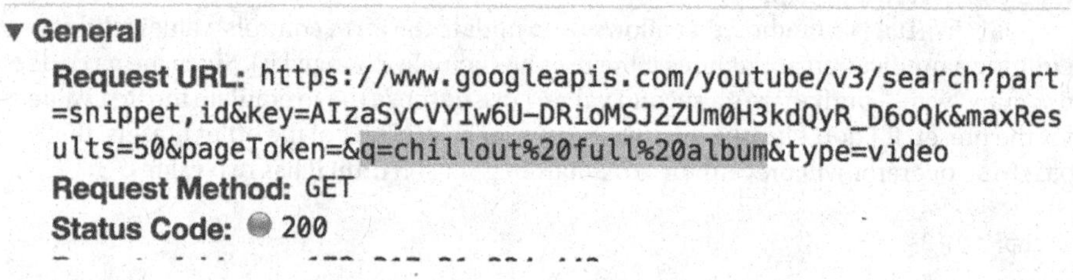

▼ **General**

Request URL: `https://www.googleapis.com/youtube/v3/search?part`
`=snippet,id&key=AIzaSyCVYIw6U-DRioMSJ2ZUm0H3kdQyR_D6oQk&maxRes`
`ults=50&pageToken=&q=chillout%20full%20album&type=video`
Request Method: `GET`
Status Code: ● `200`

Figure 7-2. *Request to YouTube's API with query parameter*

Now, we are going to view another use case that can be handled by a side-effect handler.

Trigger Search When Preset Is Changed

This step is an optional feature. However, it shows how ngrx/effects is well suited for this case and is quite easily plugged into the application features without affecting its core business.

For this feature, I added two side effects to the SEARCH_PRESET action: updatePreset and searchWithNewPreset. The following operations are needed to trigger the search feature correctly:

1. Since it's actually a new search query, we need to reset the page token.

2. Optionally, we need to reset the results array (if we would like to display results that are only relevant to the current query and preset).

3. We need to trigger a search action with the same query value.

In the following code snippet, I added two side effects that reflect the operations I just described. The first side effect implements the first two operations, while the second side effect implements the third operation and the actual search.

```
// src/app/core/effects/youtube-videos.effects.ts
@Effect()
updatePreset$ = this.actions$
  .ofType(YoutubeVideosActions.SEARCH_PRESET)
  .map(toPayload)
  .do(() => this.youtubeSearch.resetPageToken())
  .map(() => this.youtubeVideosActions.reset());

@Effect()
searchWithNewPreset$ = this.actions$
  .ofType(YoutubeVideosActions.SEARCH_PRESET)
  .map(toPayload)
  .withLatestFrom(this.store.select(state => state.videos.query))
  .map((states) => this.youtubeVideosActions.searchStart(states[1]));
```

The next section is dedicated to common solutions and enhancements that you can apply to the code.

Common Solutions

We have reviewed a lot during this book. As with every development process, there are better solutions that we can implement. "Better" in the sense that they may keep our code DRY, reusable, and perhaps easy to develop with.

In this section, I will show you several solutions that lead to a better, reusable code, as well as a few techniques and tools that you can work with to make development easier and more enjoyable.

ngrx/store Selectors

Selectors are part of a technique that involves selecting a value in the store by defining a getter function. A selector function receives an observable as an input and returns a "selectable" slice of observable from the received observable.

As the application grows, there might be a chance that a certain slice of the store is selected and used in multiple components. Also, as we have seen, a store's "slice" might change and update its structure, so having a getter function to fetch a "slice" from the store, may ensure that the correct data is returned.

Using a selector in the youtube-videos component will result in updating the code in ngOnInit using the getVideoResults$ selector. Notice that in order to use it properly, the code of the store inside the youtube-videos component is now using the let operator, which in turn "hands over" the store's observable object to the selector function.

```
// /youtube-videos.component.ts
// old implementation
ngOnInit() {
    this.videos$ = this.store.select(state => state.videos.results);
    this.setupForm();
}

// new implementation with Selector
import { EchoesState, getVideoResults$ } from '../core/store';

...

ngOnInit() {
    this.videos$ = this.store.let(getVideoResults$);
    this.setupForm();
}
```

To implement the selector function, I moved the code that selects the store's "slice" into the function getVideoResults$, which is exported from the main store/index.ts file. Currently, you will have to import the select operator from the ngrx/core package (optionally, you can add the select import within the vendor.browser.ts file).

```
import '@ngrx/core/add/operator/select';
export const getVideoResults$ = (store$: Observable<EchoesState>) => {
  return store$.select(state => state.videos.results);
};
```

This kind of selector expects an observable argument upon which the function operates. You can also create a selector for the state object that can be put in place of the function arrow selector expression getVideoResults.

```
import '@ngrx/core/add/operator/select';
const getVideoResults = (state) => state.videos.results;
export const getVideoResults$ = (store$: Observable<EchoesState>) => {
  return store$.select(getVideoResults);
};
```

To summarize, it is better to create selector functions in order to select the appropriate state from the store. It is reusable, easy to test, and may become useful when a change in the store's structure is required.

Explicitly Get State with the "take()" Operator

Although this book's premise is using reactive programming, there are situations in which we may need to explicitly get a onetime value from the store in order to use it in some cases.

For that, we may use the RxJS take(number) operator. This operator takes a number as a parameter that indicates the number of values the stream should emit. So, in the case of retrieving a onetime value, we may do the following:

```
this.videos$.take(1).subscribe(videos => {
    this.userService.saveVideosSearchHistory(videos);
});
```

However, in order to keep on using reactive programming, it is better to think of the task in terms of actions and side effects. Since this operator runs the subscription function "N" times, there's no need to unsubscribe from this observable.

Tracking State with ngrx store-devtools Extension

This tool is useful for development. It relies on Redux Devtools and allows you to watch the store's state at any time, see which actions are dispatched along with its payload, undo actions, and much more.

After setting up the store-devtool module, you will be able to open a new panel in the devtools, which should display similar to Figure 7-3.

Figure 7-3. ngrx-devtools panel

Before setting up this module, you will have to install Redux Devtools as a browser extension, available through https://github.com/zalmoxisus/redux-devtools-extension (there's a link to Chrome store).

Install the package of store-devtools with npm i @ngrx/store-devtools --save-dev. Next, add the StoreDevtoolsModule import to the app/core/store/index.ts file:

```
import { StoreDevtoolsModule } from '@ngrx/store-devtools';
```

To make sure this module will only load when the extension is available, we can use the instrumentOnlyWithExtension() method. Notice that in order to add this module only in development mode, I created an array of optional modules imports, which is included after the store's import. It's important to include the devtools modules only after the store module has been imported.

```
const optionalImports = [];
if ('production' !== ENV) {
  // Note that you must instrument after importing StoreModule
  optionalImports.push(StoreDevtoolsModule.instrumentOnlyWithExtension());
}
@NgModule({
  imports: [
    StoreModule.provideStore(reducers),
    ...optionalImports
  ]
  ...
})
```

The instrumentOnlyWithExtension() method takes an optional options configuration object as an argument. You can set the "size" of history for logging actions throughout time with the maxAge property. You can also set a monitor reducer with the monitor property and create a custom monitor to log and display the data stream.

How to Inspect the Store with Log Monitor

Using the devtools extension, we can inspect the store any time and see what values are stored at any given time. A "given time" is tied to an action that was dispatched and might have changed the store.

When the extension's panel is opened, we can select the "Log monitor" option from the top-right dropdown menu to navigate to this timeline actions view. This view displays a list of actions with a snapshot of the store after applying each action, as well as displays the action's payload (if it exists). In Figure 7-4, we can see the store's initial state after the first @ngrx/store/init action has been dispatched (this is an internal ngrx/store action).

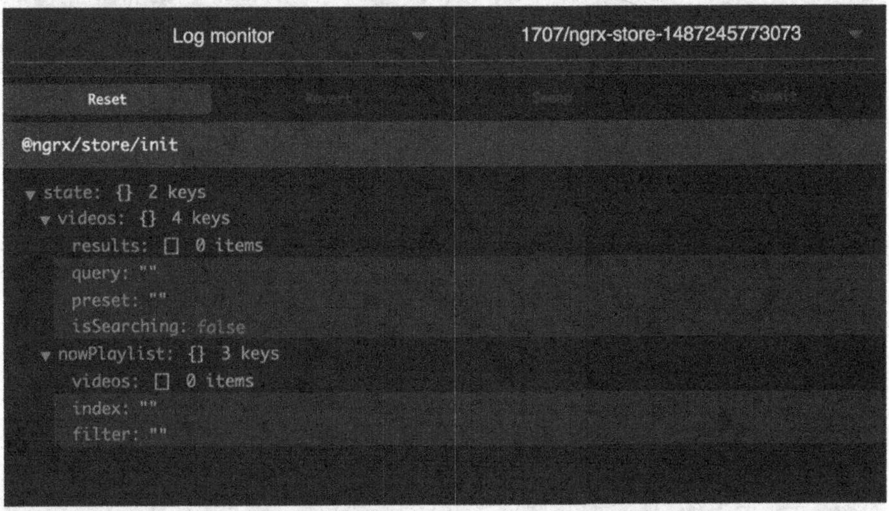

Figure 7-4. *The initial state logged to the log monitor*

In Figure 7-5, we can see the actions that were dispatched in response to a search action.

Log monitor	▼		1707/ngrx-store-1487245773073	▼
Reset	Revert			Commit

```
@ngrx/store/init

▼ state: {} 2 keys
  ▼ videos: {} 4 keys
    results: [] 0 items
    query: ""
    preset: ""
    isSearching: false
  ▼ nowPlaylist: {} 3 keys
    videos: [] 0 items
    index: ""
    filter: ""

[YoutubeVideos] SEARCH_NEW_QUERY

▼ action: {} 1 key
  payload: "ozric tentacles"

▼ state: {} 2 keys
  ▶ videos: {} 4 keys
  ▶ nowPlaylist: {} 3 keys

[YoutubeVideos] RESET

▼ state: {} 2 keys
  ▶ videos: {} 4 keys
  ▶ nowPlaylist: {} 3 keys

[YoutubeVideos] SEARCH_START
```

Figure 7-5. *Search action and side effects actions logged to the log monitor*

Aside from displaying the actions, the store, and the action's payload, the log monitor is quite interactive. One of the nice features it has that is useful for debugging is being able to disable past actions and witness how it affects the UI.

To achieve that, you simply click on the action to disable it. This will hide the store's state snapshot of this action, and the action will be struck through. Changes will be reflected in the UI, assuming the state is connected correctly to the store. In Figure 7-6 you can see that I disabled the ADD_VIDEOS action, and the UI displays an empty view.

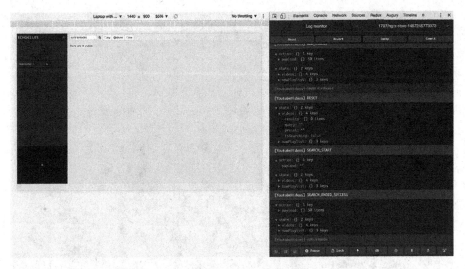

Figure 7-6. *Disabled action and how it is affecting the view*

How to Inspect the Store with Inspector

The devtools extension includes another view with which to inspect the store and timeline of actions. The "Inspector" option displays a rather different view of the store and its actions timeline.

For starters, it is divided into two sections, as shown in Figure 7-7. The left section is a list of actions that are logged. The right section includes four views for inspecting the store's state, the action's payload, the difference of the current action's payload and the previous payload that was substitued, and even an embedded code editor for generating a unit test.

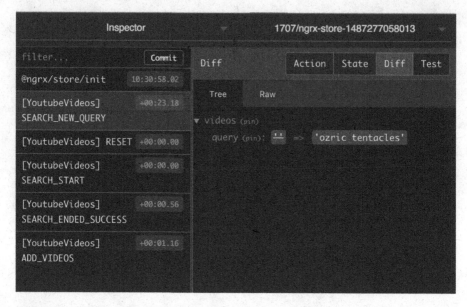

Figure 7-7. *The Inspector view*

This view is also interactive and allows you to disable an action, search and filter actions, as well as view the raw data for each option within the right panel.

Prevent Memory Leaks with Store Subscriptions

Up until now we have subscribed to the store using the async operator within templates. There might be cases where we would have to subscribe to a store's updates and perhaps perform operations that are not necessarily related only to the view. In these cases, we need to make sure to unsubscribe from any store subscriptions we have made. Usually, the best time to unsubscribe is within the ngOnDestroy life-cycle hook.

To make it easy to manage, you can create a property of the array of subscriptions. With this array property, it will be easy to iterate through the subscription elements and unsubscribe from any manual subscriptions we have made within a component.

```
ngOnInit() {
    this.videos$ = this.store.let(getVideoResults$);
    this.subscriptions.push(this.videos$.subscribe((videos) => {
        this.logService(videos);
        this.processVideos(videos);
        this.notifyService(videos);
    }));
    this.setupForm();
}
```

```
ngOnDestroy() {
    this.subscriptions.forEach(sub => sub.unsubscribe())
}
```

Connecting Store with Reactive Forms

Although reactive forms do provide a functional approach for subscribing to changes within a form, it is not yet possible to bind a property to a reactive form and get the form updated once this property value has changed.

The way to achieve that is by using a rather declarative approach where we can subscribe to the store and manually update the form. In our application, if we update the preset from another UI control, there is no implementation that will update the presets button group. A good example of such a feature would be an "undo" button that cancels the previous action and reverts to the previously saved state (actually, this is available via the store-devtools extension).

In order to support this, we can add the following code to the youtube-videos component in the ngOnInit life cycle. I added a select statement, which subscribes to the videos state within the store and subscribes to every change. I'm using the searchForm.patchValue() method in order to update the "preset" control. In order to keep it from submitting an event, I passed the optional configuration of { emitEvent: false }.

```
ngOnInit() {
    this.videos$ = this.store.let(getVideoResults$);
    this.setupForm();
    this.preset$ = this.store.select(state => state.videos.preset)
      .subscribe(preset => {
        this.searchForm.patchValue({ preset }, { emitEvent: false });
      });
}
```

Notice that since we are subscribing manually to the store, we need to remember to unsubscribe from it on the ngOnDestroy life cycle.

At the time of writing this book, there is a discussion going on about improving the reactive forms experience within the ngrx team. You can view this discussion at the Github repository of the ngrx/core library: https://github.com/ngrx/core/issues/12.

Sync Store's State to Local Storage

As some web applications' requirements are built with an offline-first approach, it may become useful to save the store's state (or part of it) to the browser's local storage. There are a few ways to connect the store to a local storage solution—using localstorage and indexedBb.

There are a few packages that add support for synchronizing the store's state to the browser's local storage. I'm going to use the npm package ngrx-store-localstorage. It's quite simple to set up and integrates seamlessly with the store.

To install the package, run this in the terminal (command line):

```
npm i ngrx-store-localstorage --save-dev
```

Next, the localStorageSync function is imported from this package within the app/core/store/index.ts file. This function receives a few arguments, as follows:

1. Keys array – an array of strings. Each string represents a store's "slice" that we would like to sync to the local storage.

2. Rehydrate Boolean – If you would like to pull the initial state from the local storage on startup, set it to true (the default is false).

3. Storage – You can hand over a storage object that conforms to the Local Storage interface. The default is Local Storage.

```
import { localStorageSync } from 'ngrx-store-localstorage';
const composeStore = compose(
  localStorageSync(['videos', 'player', 'nowPlaylist', 'search'], true),
  combineReducers
)(reducers);
```

That is all that must be done in order to sync the store's state to local storage. The state is synched with every dispatched action.

Simpler Action Creators

The action creator functions that we have defined thus far show a pattern for creating the same data structure.

In order to keep the code minimal and following the DRY principle, I created an npm module that allows you to declare action creators with minimal function declaration and type support.

To install this package, run this in the terminal:

```
npm i ngrx-action-creator-factory
```

Next, if you want to use the factory with dependency-management support, import the ActionCreatorFactory into the application's module pipes array (or any other module). Otherwise, you can just import the factory function into any actions file.

To use it, you should assign a member with the ActionCreatorFactory.create() method, which takes an action name (string) as the first and only value. You can define a type for the payload with the create method using intersection types. It is assumed that the payload will be only one argument, which may include any data relevant to the action (this follows the principle of an event object in Ecmascript as well):

```
updateIndexByMedia = ActionCreatorFactory.create<string>(NowPlaylistActions.
UPDATE_INDEX);
```

Making Reducers AOT Compatible

The Ahead of Time (AOT) compiler creates a statically ready code to run in the browser. This means that when the application runs in the browser, the compilation phase is not needed. On the contrary, compiling without AOT is JIT—Just in Time—where code is compiled at runtime, within the browser.

There are a few benefits to compiling with AOT, as follows:

1.   Less code in the final production bundles

2.   Faster rendering, as the code is ready to use

3.   Template's errors are caught in compile time

4.   Better security – HTML injection is prevented since templates are compiled to code.

There are two guidelines that we need to follow in order to update the code in our application to make it AOT compatible.

Guideline 1: Use Function Declarations for Reducers

Up until now, we have defined reducers using anonymous function assignments to variables. To make sure a reducer is AOT compatible, there are few rules to follow. First, AOT doesn't support ES6 "arrow" function exports - known as function expression or "named" function expression. Reducers must be declared with as a named "function" declaration:

```
// variable anonymous function assignment
export const videos: ActionReducer<EchoesVideos> = (
  state: EchoesVideos = initialState,
  action: Action
  ) => {
...
};

// reducer declared with the "function" keyword
export function videos (state: EchoesVideos = initialState, action: Action)
{...}
```

This will ensure the reducers can be statically analyzed by the AOT compiler.

Guideline 2: Update ngrx/effects Definition

For updating the ngrx/effects code, there are several updates we need to do. Exporting with the "default" keyword is not compatible with the AOT compiler. We need to update the code in the core/effects/index.ts file:

```
// OLD CODE
export default [
  YoutubeVideosEffects,
  NowPlaylistEffects
];

// NEW CODE
export const AppEffects = [
  YoutubeVideosEffects,
  NowPlaylistEffects
];
```

The next step is creating the effects classes one by one rather than generating them dynamically. We need to update the relevant code in the core/index.ts file as follows:

```
// OLD CODE
import effects from './effects';

@NgModule({
  imports: [
    InfiniteScrollModule,
    CommonModule,
    ReactiveFormsModule,
    CoreStoreModule,
    ...effects.map(effect => EffectsModule.run(effect)),
  ],
..
})

// NEW CODE
import { AppEffects } from './effects';

const AppEffectsModules = [
  EffectsModule.run(AppEffects[0]),
  EffectsModule.run(AppEffects[1])
];

@NgModule({
  imports: [
    InfiniteScrollModule,
    CommonModule,
    ReactiveFormsModule,
```

```
    CoreStoreModule,
    ...AppEffectsModules
  ],
```

As a last note, there's a tsconfig-aot.json configuration file that should be created. It should include a configuration that tells the compiler-cli (the tool that compiles the code with AOT) to store the AOT in a dedicated folder and prevent the compiler from generating metadata files with the compiled application. As of the time of writing this book, the AngularClass team is updating the boilerplate code to support AOT compiling.

For a more thorough guide and further explanations, I suggest that you review the full guide at https://angular.io/docs/ts/latest/cookbook/aot-compiler.html.

ngrx Code Conventions

There are a few code conventions that I follow when writing code with Angular and ngrx. These conventions lead to a consistency in the code. The following conventions are just suggestions that you might want to follow.

Action Names

An action that is handled in a reducer (and NOT only in a side effect) should describe the operation that is about to happen. This is usually composed of a verb and a noun (might be optional): VERB_NOUN as in QUEUE_VIDEOS.

Action Names for Side Effects

An action that is handled in a side effect and describes an event (such as "success") may add the "event" meaning to the verb: VERB_NOUN_EVENT as in SEARCH_ENDED_SUCCESS.

Action Creator Names

An action creator should follow the action's name so it's easier to find or skim the code that handles the same name of action: queueVideos() handles QUEUE_VIDEOS.

Store Selectors

Earlier in this chapter, I talked about defining reusable function selectors for selecting a "slice" from the store's state. There are two types of selectors:

1. Function selectors that get the store and return an observable

2. Function selectors that get a state object and return a slice of it

As a convention, a selector that returns an observable is named with the following pattern: getNOUN$ as in getVideoResults$. A selector that returns a slice of the state is simply named without the "$" suffix: getNOUN as in getVideoResults.

You can use the "reselect" library to optimize selector functions, compose "meta" selectors together, and have "memoized" states ready to use at https://github.com/reactjs/reselect.

Summary

In the beginning of this chapter, I introduced the reactive forms module and showed how to connect it to our application and replace the regular forms module we have used thus far.

In the second section of this chapter, I talked about various common challenges and their solutions when working with ngrx extensions and Angular.

This concludes the development journey for creating a web application using reactive programming with Angular and ngrx. As you can see, there are various approaches for managing state. As you can understand by now, reactive programming goes beyond code implementation. When writing reactive code you should view the application's life cycle as a continuous living app that changes through time and reacts to these changes, right here, right now. That's another perspective to take.

As a word of advice from me to you: before approaching code development, make sure you understand the challenge or the problem, design the solution (writing tests may assist greatly in this process), apply common sense, and design the implementation.

I believe the following sentence describes one's state of mind when approaching challenges - "In the **beginner's mind there are many possibilities**, in the expert's mind there are few." (Shunryu Suzuki)

If you have any questions about the subjects in this book, please feel free to contact me via http://orizens.com. You can also follow me on Twitter or Github via @orizens.

Make sure you love what you do, enjoy it, and keep on exploring.

Index

A

Action Creator Names, 143
Action creators, 38
AfterContentInit() life cycle, 91
Ahead of time (AOT) compiler, 141
Angular
    action argument, 8
    application structure, 4
    development environment, 3
    IDE/Code Editor, 4
    ngrx/effects module, 8
Angular, 10
Angular application structure, 4
AngularClass boilerplate, 28
Angularterminal and command line, 3
Angular v2, 1
app.component.ts, 23
app.module.ts, 23
Augury
    core directories, 5
    ngrx, 7
    ngrx/store, 7
    ngrx/store-log-monitor, 9
    RxJS library, 6
    terminal/command line, 3
    version control and deployment, 3
Augury Dev Tools Extension, 1

B

beforeEach function, 96
beforeEach(), 116
beforeEach() life-cycle, 95
Behavior-driven development (BDD), 94
BehaviorSubject, 37
Boilerplate

app directory, 23
config directory, 14
core directory, 23
directories structure, 14
effects directory, 25
module setting, 19
node settings, 20
output setting, 20
package, 14
Plugins, 20
resolve, 18
services directory, 26
store directory, 24

C

Change-detection strategy, 67–68
Chrome's Developer Tools, 2, 9
Code editors, 4
Command-line interface, 28
CoreStoreModule, 40
CreateApi() method, 89
CreatePlayer() method, 90

D

describe() statement, 94
devtool, 21
devtools extension, 137

E

Echoes Player (Lite)., 9
Echoes project, 52
EchoesVideos, 45
Effect's Stream, 112
Empty boilerplate awaiting, 28

■ F, G, H, I

■ J

■ K

■ L

■ M

■ N

■ O

■ P, Q

■ R

■ Y, Z

YouTube API Factory, 78
YoutubeApiFactory class, 94
YoutubeApiFactory object, 95
Youtube-list component, 74
YouTube's API, 130
YouTube search results, 74

YouTube search
    service, 75, 104, 112
YouTube Video Info Service, 79
Youtube-videos, 41–42
Youtube-videos component, 60, 103
YoutubeVideosInfo, 81
YouTube videos reducer, 41

Get the eBook for only $5!

Why limit yourself?

With most of our titles available in both PDF and ePUB format, you can access your content wherever and however you wish—on your PC, phone, tablet, or reader.

Since you've purchased this print book, we are happy to offer you the eBook for just $5.

To learn more, go to http://www.apress.com/companion or contact support@apress.com.

Apress®

Printed in the United States
By Bookmasters